COWBOY POETRY

A GATHERING

COWBOY POETRY

A GATHERING

Edited and with an
Introduction by

Hal Cannon

Gibbs M. Smith, Inc.
Peregrine Smith Books
Salt Lake City

Copyright © 1985 by Gibbs M. Smith, Inc.

A Peregrine Smith Book

Published by Gibbs M. Smith, Inc.
P. O. Box 667
Layton, Utah 84041

Book design by J. Scott Knudsen
Cover art by Carrie Henrie

Library of Congress Cataloging in Publication Data
Main entry under title:

Cowboy poetry.

   Bibliography: p.
   1. Folk poetry, American. 2. Cowboys—Poetry.
I. Cannon, Hal, 1948-
PS477.5.C67C68   1985   811'.044'08352636   85-10833

ISBN 0-87905-208-2 (pbk.)

96 95 94 93   12 13 14 15 16

CONTENTS

INTRODUCTION

Just as cowboy poetry itself corrals spirit into form, this book is the tangible product of over a year's intensive fieldwork by folklorists and researchers throughout the western United States. The poems collected here are both old and new, but they all express an honest spirit which is lean and hard; and their form – the printed words, their rhythm and rhyme as transliterated from the oral – is broken, like a fresh horse, into a manageable gait.

It was pioneer folklorists John Lomax and Howard (Jack) Thorp who first chronicled the songs and poems of the cowboys. Thorp's *Songs of the Cowboys* in 1908, and Lomax's *Cowboy Songs and other Frontier Ballads* in 1910, transcribed the most common verse in the cowboy tradition. They were followed by another Lomax volume, *Songs of the Cattle Trail and Cowboy Camps*, in 1919.

After these early gatherings, however, it was not until the middle of the century that a new look was taken at the genre. From the 1940s through the 1960s folklorists Austin and Alta Fife provided readers with additional poems and commentary, followed by Glenn Ohrlin who offered a working cowboy's insights into the art form, and then, in the last decade, by former radio cowboy singers Jim Bob Tinsley and John I. White who published further historical documentation.

This anthology of annotated poems, along with an extensive bibliography for those interested in additional reading, is thus the culmination of this twentieth century interest in cowboy poetry. In some ways it parallels Lomax's 1919 volume: in it the enduring quality of more traditional work has been complemented, through thorough field research, with the poems of many present-day working cowboys and ranchers.

Our book begins with classic poems that have proven their vitality by their longevity, surviving tenaciously in the minds and hearts of cowboys and ranchers of the West for decades. Yet approximately two-thirds of the book is devoted to contemporary poets and their poems. The sources are tapes of recitations, manuscripts sent from all over the West, and a collection of more than one hundred and fifty published works listed in the bibliography.

At the heart of cowboy poetry is the memorized performance of traditional poems. These recitations are not monotone bastards of well-known cowboy songs, but are based instead in an oral tradition of performance in both the old and new West. Each poem in this book was written to reflect a real voice, and meant to be heard aloud.

While folk poetry and formal poetry are often judged by different standards, they share the same essential literary aim; the poet is always in search of the best language, the most perfect language, for his subject matter and for his personal poetic intent. In the case of cowboy poetry this means a language which reflects light and smell and open places, hard times and soft evenings; a language coded with insider's words, special phrases and meanings, and shared values. The general form of cowboy poetry is the four-line ballad form of rhymed couplets, the same as that used by other popular poets of the nineteenth century such as Robert Service and Rudyard Kipling.

It is amazing how much cowboy poetry there is—the sheer volume of it came as a surprise to even these folklorists – considering how relatively private and isolated the tradition has been. The commercialized, stereotyped version of the cowboy life has long concealed from general view the real life of the cowboy in the West. The oral tradition of recited poetry has sustained itself almost exclusively in ranching communities, where poems have sometimes appeared in weeklies and rural interest magazines, but are mostly created – and passed around – the campfire, in the bunkhouse, and on horseback.

It is perhaps unfortunate that public and literary scholars have rarely seen beyond the television image of the cowboy. This book hopes to puncture that stereotype by allowing the cowboys to speak for themselves, as they celebrate the huge sky, the rodeo, busting broncos, the cattle drive that still goes on, the land, and the life and the times of the people who continue, spiritedly, to live that cowboy life.

Hal Cannon

ACKNOWLEDGMENTS

There could be no cowboy poetry without cowboy poets. To them and their quest for a language with which to express their lives, this book is dedicated. Special gratitude goes to all the people who allowed us into their homes to record and copy their poetry.

All of the living poets represented in this book will receive a small honorarium in gratitude for letting us use their poems. They also know that a portion of profits from this book will go for the study and encouragement of cowboy poetry.

There are countless people who worked to make this book happen. First, thanks to the team of folklorists who traveled the West to ranches to meet and befriend cowboy poets. Gary Stanton gave this project its initial and model fieldwork. Jim Griffith had the idea of studying cowboy poetry. Sarah Campsey did some of the pioneering fieldwork. Meg Glaser made the Cowboy Poetry Gathering of 1985 all come together in Elko with the help of Charles Greenhaw, Cyd McMullen Holthoff, and Lane Schulz. Thanks to Steve Siporin from the Idaho Commission on the Arts; Mike Korn from the Montana Arts Council; Carol Edison, Utah Arts Council; Liz Dear, New Mexico Museum; Warren Miller, Sharlot Hall Museum; Sharon Kahin, Buffalo Bill Historical Center; Jens Lund, Washington State Folklife Council; Pat Jasper, Texas Folklife Resources; Jim McNutt, Institute of Texan Cultures; Elaine Thatcher, Siouxland Heritage Museum; Guy Logsdon, the University of Tulsa; Greta Swenson and Drew Beisswenger, North Dakota Council on the Arts;

David Brose, Colorado Council on the Arts and Humanities; and Suzi Jones, Alaska Arts Council.

Next, thanks to the trustees, Greer Markle and Richard Hart from the Institute of the American West, a division of the Sun Valley Center for Arts and Humanities, for sponsoring this project.

Appreciation also goes to the institutions and individuals who supported this project, most notably The Folk Arts Program of the National Endowment for the Arts, Western States Arts Foundation, The Nevada Humanities Committee, the L. J. and Mary C. Skaggs Foundation, The Nevada State Council on the Arts, George Gund, Northern Nevada Community College, Elko Convention Center, Northeastern Nevada Museum.

Thanks to advisors, poets Waddie Mitchell, Drummond Hadley, Baxter Black, and Glenn Ohrlin. Book illustrations are by Fred Lambert from *Bygone Days of the Old West*, and by Lewis E. Wallis from a book of poems by Wade Lane entitled *Cowboy Meditation*. The book logo on the back cover is from *Songs of the Cowboys* (second edition, 1921) by Jack Thorp.

This old poem, like many others, has been set to a droll night herding tune. It was first published in 1885, but was undoubtedly sung and recited long before that.

THE COWBOY'S SOLILOQUY

ALLEN McCANLESS

All day o'er the prairie alone I ride,
Not even a dog to run by my side;
My fire I kindle with chips gathered round,
And boil my coffee without being ground.

Bread lacking leaven' I bake in a pot,
And sleep on the ground for want of a cot;
I wash in a puddle, and wipe on a sack,
And carry my wardrobe all on my back.

My ceiling the sky, my carpet the grass,
My music the lowing of herds as they pass;
My books are the brooks, my sermons the stones,
My parson's a wolf on a pulpit of bones.

But then if my cooking ain't very complete,
Hygienists can't blame me for living to eat;
And where is the man who sleeps more profound
Than the cowboy who stretches himself on the ground.

My books teach me constancy ever to prize,
My sermon's that small things I should not despise;
And my parson's remarks from his pulpit of bone,
Is that "the Lord favors those who look out for their own."

Between love and me lies a gulf very wide,
And a luckier fellow may call her his bride;
But Cupid is always a friend to the bold
And the best of his arrows are pointed with gold.

Friends gently hint I am going to grief,
But men must make money, and women have beef;
Society bans me a savage and dodge,
And Masons would ball me out of their lodge.

If I'd hair on my chin, I might pass for the goat,
That bore all sin in ages remote;
But why this is thusly I don't understand,
For each of the patriarchs owned a big brand.

Abraham emigrated in search of a range,
When water got scarce and he wanted a change.
Isaac had cattle in charge of Esau
And Jacob run cows for his father-in-law;
He started in business clear down at bedrock,
And made quite a fortune by watering stock.

David went from night herding and using a sling
To winning a battle and being a king;
And the shepherds when watching their flocks on the hill
Heard the message from heaven of "peace and good will."

If there is one living poet whose words have entered into cowboy tradition it is Gail Gardner, from Prescott, Arizona. "The Sierry Petes" is probably the most widely recited cowboy poem today.

THE SIERRY PETES

GAIL GARDNER

Away up high in the Sierry Petes,*
Where the yeller pines grow tall,
Ol' Sandy Bob an' Buster Jig
Had a rodeer* camp last fall.

Oh, they taken their hosses and runnin' irons
And mabbe a dawg or two,
An' they 'lowed they'd brand all the long-yered calves,
That come within their view.

And any old dogie that flapped long yeres,
An' didn't bush up* by day,
Got his long yeres whittled an' his old hide scorched,
In a most artistic way.

Now one fine day ol' Sandy Bob,
He throwed his seago* down,
"I'm sick of the smell of burnin' hair
And I 'lows I'm a-goin' to town."

So they saddles up an' hits 'em a lope,
Fer it warn't no sight of a ride,
And them was the days when a buckeroo
Could ile up his inside.

Oh, they starts her in at the Kaintucky Bar,
At the head of Whisky Row,
And they winds up down by the Depot House,
Some forty drinks below.

They then sets up and turns around,
And goes her the other way,
An' to tell you the Gawd-forsaken truth
Them boys got stewed that day.

As they was a-ridin' back to camp,
A-packin' a pretty good load,
Who should they meet but the Devil himself,
A-prancin' down the road.

Sez he, "You ornery cowboy skunks,
You'd better hunt yer holes,
Fer I've come up from Hell's Rim Rock
To gather in yer souls."

Sez Sandy Bob, "Old Devil be damned,
We boys is kinda tight,
But you aint a-goin' to gather no cowboy souls
'Thout you has some kind a fight."

So Sandy Bob punched a hole in his seago
And he swang her straight and true,
He lapped it on to the Devil's horns,
An' he taken his dallies* too.

Now Buster Jig was a riata* man
With his gut-line coiled up neat,
So he shaken her out an' he built him a loop
An' he lassed the Devil's hind feet.

Oh, they stretched him out an' they tailed him down
While the irons was a-gettin' hot,
They cropped and swaller-forked* his yeres,
Then they branded him up a lot.

They pruned him up with a de-hornin' saw
an' they knotted his tail fer a joke,
They then rid off and left him there,
Necked to a Black-Jack oak.

If you're ever up high in the Sierry Petes
An' you hear one Hell of a wail,
You'll know it's that Devil a-bellerin' around
About them knots in his tail.

Sierry Petes the Sierra Prieta Mountain range near Prescott, Arizona
rodeer Spanish for "rounding up." A rodeer camp is a round-up out on the range
bush up hide in the bushes
seago loose hemp rope
dallies transliterated from the Spanish *dale vueltas*, a Mexican term which means "give it some twists," and refers to the practice of looping rope loosely (rather than tying "hard and fast") around the saddle horn
riata Spanish for rope
swaller-forked to make an identifying notch in the ear of cattle, in the shape of a swallowtail

THE DUDE WRANGLER

GAIL GARDNER

I'll tell you a sad, sad story
Of how a cowboy fell from grace.
Now really this is something awful,
There never was so sad a case.

One time I had myself a pardner,
I never knowed one half so good;
We throwed our outfits in together
And lived the way that cowboys should.

He savvied all about wild cattle
And he was handy with a rope.
For a gentle well-reined pony,
Just give me one that he had broke.

He never owned no clothes but Levis,
He wore them until they was slick,
And he never wore no great big Stetson
'Cause where we rode the brush was thick.

He never had no time for women,
So bashful and so shy was he,
Besides he knowed that they was poison
And so he always let them be.

Well he went to work on distant ranges;
I did not see him for a year.
But then I had no cause to worry,
For I knowed that some day he'd appear.

One day I rode in from the mountains
A-feelin' good and steppin' light,
For I had just sold all my yearlins
And the price was out of sight.

But soon I seen a sight so awful
It caused my joy to fade away.
It filled my very soul with sorrow.
I never will forget that day.

For down the street there come a-walkin'
My oldtime pardner as of yore,
And although I know you will not believe me,
Let me tell you what he wore.

He had his boots outside his britches;
They was made of leather, green and red.
His shirt was of a dozen colors,
Loud enough to wake the dead.

Around his neck he had a 'kerchief,
Knotted through a silver ring;
I swear to Gawd he had a wrist-watch,
Who ever heard of such a thing?

Sez I, "Old scout now what's the trouble?
You must have et some loco weed.
If you will tell me how to help you
I'll git you anything you need."

Well he looked at me for half a minute,
And then he begin to bawl;
He sez, "Bear with me while I tell you
What made me take this awful fall.

"It was a woman from Chicago
Who put the Injun sign on me;
She told me that I was romantic,
And just as handsome as could be."

Sez he, "I'm 'fraid that there ain't nothin'
That you can do to save my hide,
I'm wranglin' dudes instead of cattle,
I'm what they call a first-class guide.

"Oh I saddles up their pump-tailed ponies,
I fix their stirrups for them, too.
I boost them up into their saddles, and
They give me tips when I am through.

"It's just like horses eatin' loco,
You can not quit it if you try.
I'll go on wranglin' dudes forever,
Until the day that I shall die."

So I drawed my gun and throwed it on him,
I had to turn my face away.
I shot him squarely through the middle,
And where he fell I left him lay.

I shorely hated for to do it,
For things that's done you cain't recall,
But when a cowboy turns dude wrangler,
He ain't no good no more at all.

THE ZEBRA DUN*

ANONYMOUS

We were camped on the plains at the head of the Cimarron
When along came a stranger who stopped to arger some.
He looked so very foolish that we began to look around,
We thought he was a greenhorn that had just 'scaped
        from town.

We asked if he'd been to breakfast; he hadn't had a smear;
So we opened up the chuckbox and bade him have his share.
He took a cup of coffee and some biscuits and some beans,
Then began to talk and tell about foreign kings and queens,

About the Spanish War and fighting on the seas
With guns as big as steers and ramrods big as trees,
And about old Paul Jones, a mean-fighting son of a gun
Who was the grittiest cuss that ever pulled a gun.

Such an educated feller, his thoughts just came in herds,
He astonished all them cowboys with them jawbreaking words.
He just kept on talking till he made the boys all sick,
And they began to look around just how to play a trick.

He said he had lost his job upon the Santa Fe
And was going across the plains to strike the 7-D.
He didn't say how come it, some trouble with the boss,
But said he'd like to borrow a nice fat saddle hoss.

This tickled all the boys; they laughed way down
            In their sleeves,
"We will lend you a horse just as fresh and fat as you please."
Shorty grabbed a lariat and roped the Zebra Dun
And turned him over to the stranger and waited for the fun.

Ol' Dunny was a rocky outlaw that had grown awful wild,
He could paw the white out of the moon every jump
            for a mile.
Ol' Dunny stood right still,as if he didn't know,
Until he was saddled and ready for to go.

When the stranger hit the saddle, Ol' Dunny quit the earth
And traveled right straight up for all that he was worth.
A-pitching and a-squealing, a-having wall-eyed fits,
His hind feet perpendicular, his front ones in the bits.

We could see the tops of the mountains under Dunny's
            every jump,
But the stranger he was growed there just like the
            camel's hump.
The stranger sat upon him and curled his black mustache,
Just like a summer boarder waiting for his hash.

He thumped him in the shoulders and spurred him
            when he whirled
To show them flunky punchers that he was the wolf
            of the world.
When the stranger had dismounted once more
            upon the ground,
We knew he was a thoroughbred and not a gent from town.

The boss, who was standing round watching the show
Walked right up to the stranger and told him he needn't go.
"If you can use the lasso like you rode old Zebra Dun,
You are the man I've been looking for ever since the year one."

Oh, he could twirl the lariat, and he didn't do it slow;
Could catch them feet nine out of ten for any kind of dough.
One thing and a shore thing I've learned since I've been born,
Every educated feller ain't a plumb greenhorn.

Dun a buckskin-colored horse

This anonymous poem is not recited much anymore since people quit calling the bicycle a "wheel."

THE GOL-DARNED WHEEL

ANONYMOUS

I can ride the wildest bronco in the wild and woolly West,
I can rake him, I can break him, let him do his level best.
I can handle any cattle ever wore a coat of hair,
And I've had a lively tussle with a tarnal grizzly bear.
I can rope and throw a longhorn of the wildest Texas brand,
And at Injun disagreements I can take a leading hand.
But I finally met my master, and he really made me squeal,
When the boys got me astraddle of that gol-darned wheel.

'Twas a tenderfoot who brought it while he was on his way
From this land of freedom out to San Francisco Bay.
He tied it at the ranch house to get outside a meal,

Never dreaming that us cowboys would monkey with his
        gol-darned wheel.
There was old Arizona and there was Jack Magill,
They said I'd been a-braggin' way too much about my skill.
They said I'd find myself against a different kind of deal
If I would get astraddle of that gol-darned wheel.

Such a slam against my talent made me madder than a mink,
And I swore that I would ride it for amusement or for chink,
That it was just a plaything for the kids and such about,
And they'd have their idees shattered if they'd lead
        the critter out.
They held it while I mounted and I gave the word to go.
The shove they gave to start me warn't unreasonably slow,
But I never spilt a cussword and I never give a squeal,
I was buildin' reputation on that gol-darned wheel.

The grade was mighty sloping from the ranch
        down to the creek,
And I went a-gallyflutin' like a crazy lightning streak,
Just a-whizzing and a-dartin', first this way and then that,
The darned contrivance wobbling like the flying of a bat.
I pulled up on the handles but I couldn't check it up,
I yanked and sawed and hollered, but the darn thing
        wouldn't stop.
And then a sort of meechin' in my brain began to steal
That the Devil had a mortgage on that gol-darned wheel.

I've a sort of dim and hazy remembrance of the stop,
With the world a-goin' round and the stars all tangled up.
Then there came an intermission that lasted till I found
I was lying at the bunkhouse with the boys all gathered round.
And a doctor was a-sewing on the skin where it was ripped,
And old Arizona whispered, "Well, old boy, I guess
        you're whipped."
I said that "I am busted from sombrero down to heel."
He grinned and said, "You ort to see that gol-darned wheel!"

S. Omar Barker came from a ranching family and had a successful writing career for many years. He lived in Las Vegas, New Mexico, until he passed away in the spring of 1985.

RAIN ON THE RANGE

S. OMAR BARKER

When your boots are full of water and your hat brim's
       all a-drip,
And the rain makes little rivers dribblin' down your
       horse's hip,
When every step your pony takes, it purt near bogs him down,
It's then you git to thinkin' of them boys that work in town.
They're maybe sellin' ribbon, or they're maybe slingin' hash,
But they've got a roof above 'em when the thunder
       starts to crash.
They do their little doin's, be their wages low or high,
But let it rain till hell's a pond, they're always warm and dry.
Their beds are stuffed with feathers, or at worst with
       plenty straw,
While your ol' soggy soogans* may go floatin' down the draw.
They've got no rope to fret about that kinks up when it's wet;
There ain't no puddle formin' in the saddle where they set.
There's womenfolks to cook 'em up the chuck they
       most admire
While you gnaw cold, hard biscuits 'cause the cook can't
       build a fire.

When you're ridin' on the cattle range and hit a rainy spell,
Your whiskers git plumb mossy, and you note a mildewed smell
On everything from leather to the makin's in your sack;
And you git the chilly quivers from the water down your back.
You couldn't pull your boots off if you hitched 'em to a mule;
You think about them ribbon clerks, and call yourself a fool

For ever punchin' cattle with a horse between your knees,
Instead of sellin' ribbons and a-takin' of your ease.
You sure do git to ponderin' about them jobs in town,
Where slickers ain't a-drippin' when the rain comes
        sluicin' down.
It's misery in your gizzard, and you sure do aim to quit,
And take most any sheltered job you figger you can git.
But when you've got your neck all bowed to quit
        without a doubt,
The rain just beats you to it, and the sun comes bustin' out!
Your wet clothes start to steamin', and most everywhere
        you pass
You notice how that week of rain has livened up the grass.
That's how it is with cowboys when a rainy spell is hit:
They hang on till it's over—then there ain't no need to quit!

soogans or sougan, a quilt or comforter in a cowboy's bedrole

BEAR ROPIN' BUCKAROO

S. OMAR BARKER

Now ropin' bears (says Uncle Sid) is sure a heap of fun,
And a lot more gizzard-thrillin' than to shoot 'em with a gun.
I roped a big ol' he one time when I was young and raw.
He must have weighed five hundred pounds, and monstrous
        was his paw.
He'd wandered out upon the flats for cowchip bugs and such.
Them grubs and worms suit a bear like pretzels
        suit the Dutch.
I purt near didn't ketch him, for a bear can split the breeze,
And your pony's got to wiggle if he beats him to the trees.
But the roan* that I was ridin', he was tough and mighty fleet.
He overhauled ol' bruin, and my loop was quick and neat.
It ketched him snug around the neck, and when he
        hit the end
I heard the cinches stretchin', and I felt the saddle bend!
My pony put the brakes on till he sure 'nuff plowed
        the ground.
It purt near made me sorry that there wern't no crowd around
To watch a salty hand like me demonstrate my skill
At learnin' Mister Bruin to obey my wish and will!

"Come on, ol' b'ar!" I bellered. "You're a wild and woolly scamp,
But I'm the apparatus that can lead you into camp!"
At first I feared the rope would bust. I'd lose him if it should.
About a minute later, boys, I wished to hell it would!
That bear r'ared up and popped his teeth –'twas like a
        pistol crack–
Then grabbed my rope hand over hand and come right
        up the slack.
I give a squall and swung my hat to slap him in the eyes,
But a he-bear ain't a critter that it's easy to surprise.

My pony tried to quit me, but he had a bear in tow,
And a-clingin' to the saddle was a load he couldn't throw.
He got a-straddle of the rope, a log, a bush, a bear.
He wallered on his haunches, and he pawed the upper air.
Ol' bruin's jaws and paws and claws, they purt near
        had me skun.
My rope was anchored to the horn and wouldn't
        come undone.
Seemed like we fought for hours, and I couldn't see no hope,
When bruin bit my twine in two and quit us on the lope.

roan a grayish-yellow or reddish-brown horse with spots of gray or white
thickly interspersed

JACK POTTER'S COURTIN'

S. OMAR BARKER

Now young Jack Potter was a man who knowed the
        ways of steers,
From burr-nests in their hairy tails to ticks that chawed
        their ears.
A Texican and cowhand, to the saddle bred and born,
He could count a trail herd on the move and never
        miss a horn.
But one day on a tally, back in eighteen eighty-four,
He got to actin' dreamy, and he sure did miss the score.
The Old Man knowed the symptoms. "Jack, you ain't no
        good like this.
I'll give you just ten days to go and find out what's amiss!"
A "miss" was just what ailed him, for he'd fell in love for sure
With a gal named Cordie Eddy, mighty purty, sweet and pure.

So now Jack rode a hundred miles, a-sweatin' with the thought
Of sweetsome words to ask her with, the way a feller ought:
"I'm just a humble cowhand, Miss Cordie, if you please,
That hereby asks your heart and hand upon my
                    bended knees!"
It sounded mighty simple, thus rehearsed upon the trail,
But when he come to Cordie's house, his words all
                    seemed to fail.
'Twas "Howdy, Ma'am, an' how's the crops? An' how's your
                    Pa an' Ma?"
For when it come to askin' her, he couldn't come to taw.

He took her to a dance one night. The hoss she rode was his.
"He's a dandy little horse," she says. "Well, yep," says Jack,
                    "he is."
They rode home late together and the moon was ridin' high,
And Jack, he got to talkin' 'bout the stars up in the sky,
And how they'd guide a trail herd like they do sea-goin' ships;
But words of love and marriage, they just wouldn't pass
                    his lips.
So he spoke about the pony she was ridin', and he said:
"You'll note he's fancy gaited, an' don't never fight his head."
"He's sure a little dandy!" she agrees, and heaves a sigh.
Jack says: "Why, you can have him—that is, maybe,
                    when I die."
He figgered she might savvy what he meant, or maybe guess,
And give him that sweet answer which he longed for,
                    namely "yes."

But when they reached the ranch house he was still
                    a-wonderin' how
He would ever pop the question, and he had to do it now
Or wait and sweat and suffer till the drive was done that fall,
When maybe she'd be married and he'd lose her after all.
He put away her saddle, led his pony to the gate:
"I reckon I'll be driftin', ma'am. It's gettin' kinder late."

Her eyes was bright as starlight and her lips looked sweet
    as flow'rs.
Says Jack: "Now this here pony—is he mine, or is he *ours?*"
"*Our* pony, Jack!" she answered, and her voice was soft
    as moss.
Then Jack, he *claims* he kissed her—but she claims he kissed
    the hoss!

This hundred-year old poem has been pared down here to a folksong version.

THE COWBOYS' CHRISTMAS BALL

LARRY CHITTENDON

Way out in western Texas, where the Clear Fork's waters flow,
Where the cattle are a-browsin' and the Spanish ponies grow,
Where the northers come a-whistlin' from beyond the
    Neutral Strip,
And the prairie dogs are wheezin' as though they had
    the grippe,
Where lonesome, tawny prairies melt into airy streams
While the Double Mountains slumber in heav'nly
    kinds of dreams,
Where the antelope is grazin' and the lonely plovers call,
It was there that I attended the cowboys' Christmas ball.

The boys had left the ranches and come to town in piles.
The ladies, kinder scatterin', had gathered in for miles.
And yet the place was crowded, as I remember well.
'Twas gave on this occasion at the Morning Star Hotel.

The music was a fiddle and a lively tambourine,
And a viol came, imported by the stage from Abilene.
The room was togged out gorgeous with mistletoe and shawls
And the candles flickered frescoes around the airy walls.

The women folks looked lovely, the boys looked kinder treed,
Till the leader commenced yellin', "Whoa, fellers, let's
      stampede,"
And the music started sighin' and a-wailin' through the hall
As a kind of introduction to the cowboys' Christmas ball.
The leader was a feller that came from Swenson's ranch,
They called him Windy Billy from Little Deadman's Branch.
His rig was kinder keerless, big spurs and high-heeled boots.
He had the reputation that comes when fellers shoots.

His voice was like a bugle upon the mountain height.
His feet were animated and a mighty movin' sight
When he commenced to holler, "Now, fellers, stake yer pen.
Lock horns ter all them heifers and rustle them like men,
Salute yer lovely critters, now swing and let 'em go,
Climb the grapevine round 'em, now all hands do-si-do.
You maverick, jine the roundup, jes' skip the waterfall."
Huh, it was gettin' active, at the cowboys' Christmas ball.

Don't tell me 'bout cotillions, or Germans, no sir-ee!
That whirl at Anson City jes' takes the cake with me.
I'm sick of lazy shufflin's, of them I've had my fill.
Give me a frontier breakdown backed up by Windy Bill.
McAllister ain't nowhere when Windy leads the show.
I've seen 'em both in harness, and so I ought ter know.
Oh, Bill, I shan't forget yer and I oftentimes recall
That lively gaited soiree, the cowboys' Christmas ball.

T. J. (Tim) McCoy was a silent-screen cowboy star, and few people knew him as a cowboy poet who published a small pamphlet of poems while cowboying in Wyoming.

ALKALI PETE HITS TOWN

T. J. McCOY

Clear the trail, you short-horn pilgrims, hunt your hole or
       climb a tree,
Else I'll ride yu down and stomp yu in the earth.
I'm a ring-tailed he-gorilla on a hell-bent jamboree,
And I've rid to town to celebrate my birth.

I was born way over yonder on the head of Bitter Creek
Where a self-respectin' cactus couldn't dwell,
Where the gentle soothin' zephyrs that caress your
       cheek at night
Feel like a hot-box on the very hubs of hell.

I was suckled by a grizzly and was weaned on nigger gin,
Gila monsters was my playmates as a lad.
My gums turn blue by moonlight, the sparks fly off my teeth,
And in the hot midsummer dogdays, I go mad!

I'm a reptile from the desert strewn with dead
        things all around,
And the poison 'round my teeth is just a purlin'.
I'm a regular hydrophobia skunk, my tail drags on the ground,
And I'm lookin' fer some cuss to try and curl it.

Line up, gents, and name your likker, plant your hind foot on
        the rail,
Pour a quart of poison underneath your shirt.
'Fore my temper gits ta smartin' and my six-guns start a barkin'
And I smoke your golderned village off the earth.

I'm a demon from the ranges, where all livin' things is dead,
With the wolf-pack in the night, I love to prowl.
I am mean plum ta the marrer, I'm a holy howlin' terror.
I'm a he-wolf and it's my night fer to howl.

This anonymous poem is said to have been adapted from an even older logging poem.

SILVER JACK

ANONYMOUS

I was on the drive in eighty
Working under Silver Jack,
Which the same is now in Jackson
And ain't soon expected back,
And there was a fellow 'mongst us
By the name of Robert Waite;
Kind of cute and smart and tonguey.
Guess he was a graduate.

He could talk on any subject
From the Bible down to Hoyle,
And his words flowed out so easy,
Just as smooth and slick as oil.
He was what they call a sceptic,
And he loved to sit and weave
Hifalutin' words together
Tellin' what he didn't believe.

One day we all were sittin' round
Smokin' nigger head tobacco
And hearing Bob expound;
Hell, he said, was all a humbug,
And he made it plain as day
That the Bible was a fable;
And we 'lowed it looked that way.
Miracles and such like
Were too rank for him to stand,
And as for him they called the Savior
He was just a common man.

"You're a liar," someone shouted,
"And you've got to take it back."
Then everybody started,
'Twas the words of Silver Jack.
And he cracked his fists together
And he stacked his duds and cried,
"'Twas in that thar religion
That my mother lived and died;
And though I haven't always
Used the Lord exactly right,
Yet when I hear a chump abuse him
He's got to eat his words or fight."

Now, this Bob he weren't no coward
And he answered bold and free:
"Stack your duds and cut your capers,
For there ain't no flies on me."
And they fit for forty minutes
And the crowd would whoop and cheer
When Jack spit up a tooth or two,
Or when Bobby lost an ear.

But at last Jack got him under
And he slugged him onct or twict,
And straightway Bob admitted
The divinity of Christ.
But Jack kept reasoning with him
Till the poor cuss gave a yell
And 'lowed he'd been mistaken
In his views concerning hell.

Then the fierce encounter ended
And they riz up from the ground,
And someone brought a bottle out
Which he kindly passed around.
And we drank to Bob's religion
In a cheerful sort o' way,
But the spread of infidelity
Was checked in camp that day.

*Eugene Ware is said to have written this poem "way back in the 1860s"
and it comes from Walter F. Meyer's collection of cowboy poetry.*

THE BLIZZARD

EUGENE WARE

The fiddler was improvising,
At times he would cease to play,
Then shutting his eyes
He sang and sang, in a wild ecstatic way;

Then ceasing his song, he whipped and
Whipped the strings with his frantic bow,
Releasing impatient music,
Alternately loud and low;

Then wilting and reeling,
He sang as if he were dreaming aloud;
And wrapped the frenzied music
Around him like a shroud;

And this is the strange refrain,
Which he sang in a minor key:
"No matter how long the river,
The river will reach the sea!"

It was midnight at the Cimarron
Not many a year ago;
The blizzard was whirling pebbles and sand
And billows of frozen snow.

He sat on a bale of harness,
In a dugout roofed with clay;
The wolves overhead bewailed
In a dismal protracted way;

They peeped down the adobe chimney,
And quarreled and sniffed and clawed,
But the fiddler kept on with his music
As the blizzard stalked abroad;

And time and again, that strange refrain
Came forth in a minor key:
"No matter how long the river,
The river will reach the sea!"

Around him on boxes and barrels,
Uncharmed by the fiddler's tune,
The herders were drinking and
Betting their cartridges on vantoon,

And once in a while, a player,
In spirit of reckless fun,
Would join in the fiddler's music
And fire off the fiddler's gun.

An old man sat on a sack of corn
And stared with a vacant gaze;
He had lost his hopes in the Gypsum Hills,
And he thought of the olden days.

The tears fell fast when the strange refrain
Came forth in a minor key:
"No matter how long the river,
The river will reach the sea!"

At morning the tempest ended,
And the sun came back once more;
The old, old man of the Gypsum Hills
Had gone to the smokey shore.

They chopped him a grave in the frozen ground
Where the morning sunlight fell;
With a restful look he held
In his hand an invisible asphodel.*

They filled up the grave, and each herder
Said good-by, till the Judgement Day.
But the fiddler stayed, and he sang and played,
As the herders walked away

A requiem in a lonesome land,
In a mournful minor key:
"No matter how long the river,
The river will reach the sea!"

asphodel a lilly-like plant

"Windy Bill" is an old and well-known poem, sometimes also sung. This particular version comes from Ross Knox of Solignan, Arizona.

WINDY BILL

ANONYMOUS

Windy Bill was a Texas boy
And he could rope, you bet.
And he swore that the steer he couldn't tie
He hadn't met as yet.

The boys knew of an old black steer,
And a sort of bad outlaw
Who run down in the malpais*
At the foot of a rocky draw.

Now this old black steer,
He'd stood his ground with punchers from everywhere,
And the boys bet Bill two to one
That he couldn't quite get there.

So he saddled up his old grey hoss,
His back and withers raw, and
Prepared to tackle that old black brute
That run down in the draw.

With his brass all spit and his Sam Stack tree*,
And his shafts and tacks to boot,
With his old Magee* tied hard and fast
He swore he'd get that brute.

Now the first time he come a ridin' round,
This steer begin to paw,
Then he throwed his head up in the air
And went driftin' down the draw.

The old grey horse built to him,
For he'd been eatin' corn,
And Bill, he laced that old Magee
Around that black steer's horns.

The old grey horse he set up hard,
Bill's cinches snapped like straw,
And his Sam Stack tree and his old Magee
Went driftin' down the draw.

Bill lit in a flint rock pile,
His hands and face was scratched,
Says he, "Well I thought I could rope her better,
But I guess I've met my match."

He paid his debts like a little man,
Without a bit of jaw,
And allowed his old black he was the boss
Of anything in the draw.

Now there's a moral to my story, boys.
As you can plainly see,
Don't ever tie your old Magee
To your saddle tree.

But take your dallywelters*
Accordin' to California law.
And you'll never see your Sam Stack tree
Go driftin' down the draw.

malpais black volcanic rock, in Spanish literally "bad land"
Sam Stack an old style of saddle tree (the frame a saddle is constructed on)
named after an early well-known western saddle maker
Magee or Maguey, rope made of century plant fibers
dallywelters English transliteration of the Spanish *dale vuelta*, (see "Sierra
Petes")

This poem is a classic by one of the great old-time cowboy poets from Montana, D. J. O'Malley.

D-2 HORSE WRANGLER

D. J. O'MALLEY

One day I thought I'd have some fun,
And see how punching cows was done;
So, when the roundup had begun,
I tackled a cattle king;
Says he: "My foreman is in town;
He's at the MacQueen, his name is Brown;
Go over, and I think he'll take you down."
Says I: "That's just the thing."

We started for the ranch next day,
Brown talked to me most all the way,
He said cowpunching was only fun,
It was no work at all;
That all I had to do was ride,
It was just like drifting with the tide,
Geemany crimany, how he lied;
He surely had his gall.

He put me in charge of a cavard*
And told me not to work too hard,
That all I had to do was guard
The horses from getting away.
I had one hundred and sixty head,
And oft' times wished that I was dead.
When one got away Brown he turned red.
Now this is the truth, I say.

Sometimes a horse would make a break,
Across the prairie he would take
As though he were running for a stake,
For him it was only play.
Sometimes I couldn't head him at all,
And again my saddle horse would fall
And I'd speed on like a cannon ball
Till the earth came in my way.

They led me out an old gray hack
With a great big set fast on his back,
They padded him up with gunny sacks
And used my bedding all.
When I got on he left the ground
Jumped up in the air and turned around.
I busted the earth as I came down,
It was a terrible fall.

They picked me up and carried me in
And rubbed me down with a rolling pin:
"That's the way they all begin,
You are doing well," says Brown.
"And tomorrow morning if you don't die,
I'll give you another horse to try."
"Oh! won't you let me walk?" says I.
"Yes," says he. "Into town."

I've traveled up and I've traveled down,
I've traveled this country all around,
I've lived in city, I've lived in town,
And I have this much to say:
Before you try it, go kiss your wife,
Get a heavy insurance on your life,
Then shoot yourself with a butcher knife,
It's far the easiest way.

cavard from the Spanish *cavallad*, a group of saddle horses

This poem has often taken on a melody, and has been abbreviated in the oral tradition.

THE COWBOY'S DANCE SONG

JAMES BARTON ADAMS

Now you can't expect a cowboy to agitate his shanks
In the etiquettish fashion of aristocratic ranks,
When he's always been accustomed to shake the heel and toe
In the rattling ranchers' dances where much etiquette don't go.
You can bet I set there laughing in quite an excited way,
A giving of the squinters an astonished sort of play,
When I happened into Denver and was asked to take a prance
In the smooth and easy measures of a high-toned dance.

When I got among the ladies in their frocks of fleecy white,
And the dudes togged out in wrappings that was simply
                    out of sight,
Tell you what, I was embarrassed and somehow I couldn't keep
From feeling like a burro in a purty flock of sheep.
Every step I took was awkward and I blushed a flaming red,
Like the upper decorations of a turkey gobbler's head.
And the ladies said 'twas seldom they had ever had a chance
To see an old-time puncher at a high-toned dance.

I cut me out a heifer from that bunch of purty girls,
And I yanked her to the center to dance those dreamy whirls.
She laid her head upon my breast in a loving sort of way
And we drifted into heaven while the band began to play.
I could feel my neck a burning from her nose's breathing heat
As she docey-doed around me, half the time upon my feet.
She looked up into my blinkers with a soul-dissolving glance
Quite conducive to the pleasures of a high-toned dance.

Every nerve just got to dancing to the music of delight,
And I hugged that little sagehen uncomfortably tight;
But she never made a beller and the glances of her eyes
Seemed to thank me for the pleasures of a genuine surprise.
She cuddled up against me in a loving sort of way,
And I hugged her all the tighter for her trustifying play,
Tell you what, the joys of heaven ain't a cussed circumstance
To the huggamania pleasures of a high-toned dance.

When they struck the old cotillion on that music bill of fare,
Every bit of devil in me seemed to bust out on a tear;
I fetched a cowboy war whoop and I started in to rag
Till the rafters started sinking and the floor began to sag.
My partner she got sea sick, and then she staggered for a seat,
And I balanced to the next one but she dodged me
                    slick and neat.
Tell you what, I took the creases from my go-to-meeting pants
When I put the cowboy trimmings on that high-toned dance.

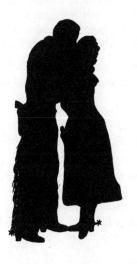

Bruce Kiskaddon is a cowboy's cowboy poet. His poems are dearly loved by ranch people all over the West. He wrote many poems which appeared through the thirties and forties.

THAT LITTLE BLUE ROAN

BRUCE KISKADDON

Most all of you boys have rode hosses like that.
He wasn't too thin but he never got fat.
The old breed that had a moustache on the lip;
He was high at the wethers and low at the hip.
His ears always up, he had wicked bright eyes
And don't you furgit he was plenty cow wise.

His ears and his fets and his pasterns* was black
And a stripe of the same run the length of his back.
Cold mornin's he'd buck, and he allus would kick,
No hoss fer a kid or a man that was sick.
But Lord what a bundle of muscle and bone;
A hoss fer a cowboy, that little blue roan.

Fer afternoon work or fer handlin' a herd,
He could turn anything but a lizzard or bird.
Fer ropin' outside how that cuss could move out.
He was to 'em before they knowed what 'twas about.
And runnin' downhill didn't faize him aytall.
He was like a buck goat and he never did fall.

One day in the foothills he give me a break,
He saved me from makin' a awful mistake.
I was ridin' along at a slow easy pace,
Takin' stock of the critters that used that place,
When I spied a big heifer without any brand.
How the boys ever missed her I don't understand.

Fer none of the stock in that country was wild,
It was like takin' candy away from a child.

She never knowed jest what I had on my mind
Till I bedded her down on the end of my twine.
I had wropped her toes up in an old hoggin' string*
And was buildin' a fire to heat up my ring.*
I figgered, you see, I was there all alone
Till I happened to notice that little blue roan.

That hoss he was usin' his eyes and his ears,
And I figgered right now there was somebody near.
He seemed to be watchin' a bunch of piñon,
And I shore took a hint from that little blue roan.

Instead of my brand, well, I run on another.
I used the same brand that was on the calf's mother.
I branded her right, pulled her up by the tail
With a kick in the rump fer to make the brute sail.
I had branded her proper and marked both her ears,
When out of the piñons two cow men appears.

They both turned the critter and got a good look
While I wrote the brand down in my old tally book.
There was nothin to do so they rode up and spoke
And we all three set down fer a sociable smoke.
The one owned the critter I'd happened to brand,
He thanked me of course and we grinned and shook hands,
Which he mightn't have done if he only had known
The warnin' I got from that little blue roan.

pasterns the part of a horses's foot between the fetlock and hoof
hoggin' string a short rope used to hogtie calves
ring a portable branding iron carried by cowboys which is then heated and
held by two green willows as this free style brand is applied.

WHEN THEY'VE FINISHED
SHIPPING CATTLE IN THE FALL

BRUCE KISKADDON

Though you're not exactly blue,
Yet you don't feel like you do
In the winter, or the long hot summer days.
For your feelin's and the weather
Seem to sort of go together,
And you're quiet in the dreamy autumn haze.
When the last big steer is goaded
Down the chute, and safely loaded;
And the summer crew has ceased to hit the ball;
When a feller starts a draggin'
To the home ranch with the wagon,
When they've finished shippin' cattle in the fall.

Only two men left a standin'
On the job for winter brandin',
And your pardner he's a loafin' at your side.
With a bran new saddle creakin',
Neither one of you is speakin',
And you feel it's goin' to be a silent ride.
But you savvy one another,
For you know him like a brother,
He is friendly but he's quiet, that is all;
  He is thinkin' while he's draggin'
  To the home ranch with the wagon—
  When they've finished shippin' cattle in the fall.

And the saddle hosses stringin'
At an easy walk a swingin'
In behind the old chuckwagon movin' slow.
They are weary, gaunt and jaded
With the mud and brush they've waded,
And they settled down to business long ago.
Not a hoss is feelin' sporty,
Not a hoss is actin' snorty;
In the spring the brutes was full of buck and bawl;
But they're gentle, when they're draggin'
To the home ranch with the wagon,
When they've finished shippin' cattle in the fall.

And the cook leads the retreat
Up there on his wagon seat,
With his hat pulled way down on his head.
Used to make that old team hustle,
Now he hardly moves a muscle,
And a feller might imagine he was dead.
'Cept his old cob pope is smokin'
As he lets his team go pokin'
Hittin' all the humps and hollers in the road.
No the cook has not been drinkin',
He's just settin' there and thinkin'
'Bout the places and the people that he knowed.
You can see the dust a trailin'
And two little clouds a sailin',
And a big mirage like lakes and timber tall.
To the home ranch with the wagon—
When they've finished shippin' cattle in the fall.

When you make the camp that night,
Though the fire is burnin' bright,
Yet nobody seems to have a lot to say.
In the spring you sung and hollered,
Now you git your supper swallered

And you crawl into your blankets right away.
Then you watch the stars a shinin'
Up there in the soft blue linin'
And you sniff the frosty night air clear and cool.
You can hear the night hoss shiftin'
And your memory starts a driftin'
To the little village where you went to school.
With its narrow gravel streets
And the kids you used to meet,
And the common where you used to play baseball.
Now you're far away and draggin'
To the home ranch with the wagon—
For they've finished shippin' cattle in the fall.

And your schoolboy sweetheart, too,
With her eyes of honest blue,
Best performer in the old home talent show.
You was nothin' but a kid
But you liked her, sure you did—
Lord! And that was over thirty years ago.
Then your memory starts to roam
From Old Mexico to Nome,
From the Rio Grande to the Powder River,
Of the things you seen and done,
Some of them was lots of fun
And a lot of other things they make you shiver.
'Bout that boy by name of Reid
That was killed in a stampede,
'Twas away up north you helped to dig his grave.
And your old friend Jim the boss
That got tangled with a hoss,
And the fellers couldn't reach in time to save.

You was there when Ed got hisn,
Boy that killed him's still in prison,
And old Lucky George is rich and livin' high.

Poor old Tom, he come off worst,
Got his leg broke, died of thirst,
Lord but that must be an awful way to die.

Then them winters at the ranches,
And the old time country dances,
Everybody there was sociable and gay.
Used to lead 'em down the middle
Jest a prancin' to the fiddle
Never thought of goin' home till the break of day.

No there ain't no chance for sleepin',
For the memories come a creepin',
And sometimes you think you hear the voices call;
When a feller starts a draggin'
To the home ranch with the wagon—
When they've finished shippin' cattle in the fall.

THE COWBOY'S DREAM

BRUCE KISKADDON

A cowboy and his trusty pal
Were camped one night by an old corral;
They were keeping a line on the boss's steers
And looking for calves with lengthy ears.
The summer work was long since through
And only the winter branding to do.
When he went to rest there was frost on his bed
But he pulled the tarp over his head,
And into his blankets he burrowed deep;
He soon got warm and was fast asleep.
He dreamed he was through with his wayward past
And had landed safe in Heaven at last.

A city was there with its pearly gate
And the golden streets were wide and straight.
The marble palaces gleamed and shone
And the choir sang 'round the great white throne.
Outside there were trees and meadows green,
Such a beautiful range he had never seen,
Great rivers of purest waters flowed
Though it never rained nor it never snowed.

He stood aside on the golden street,
There were heavy spurs on his booted feet,
His bat wing chaps were laced with whang,
But he listened and looked while the angels sang.
He noticed he was the only one
With a broad-brimmed hat and big six gun.

So he said to a saint, "I'd shore admire
To be dressed like one of that angel choir,
Instead of these chaps and spurs and gun;
And I reckon as how it could be done."

So they took him into a room aside
And they fastened wings on his toughened hide.
They fitted him out with a flowing robe,
Like the lady who looks in the crystal globe.
They gave him a crown and a golden harp
And the frost lay thick on the cowboy's tarp.

He twanged his harp and he sang awhile,
Then he thought of something that made him smile.
Said he, "I reckon these wings would do
To show some mustangs a thing or two.
I'll jump a bunch and I'll yell and whoop,
I'll kick their tails and I'll flop and swoop;
I'll light a straddle of one of the things,
And I'll flop his flanks with my angel wings.
I'll ride him bare-back, but if I fail,
And he bucks me off, I'll simply sail."
He hunted wild horses in his dream,
But all he found was the chariot team
That Old Elija drove in there,
And to pick on them would hardly be fair.

So he seated himself beneath a tree
And rested his crown upon his knee.
He watched the beautiful angels go
Flying and fluttering to and fro.
At last one landed and started to walk,
She came up close and began to talk.
She had lovely hair of golden brown
And was dressed in a flimsy silken gown.
She had dimpled cheeks, her eyes were blue,
And her fair white skin was beautiful too.

The cowboy gazed at the angel's charms
And attempted to clasp her within his arms.
"Stop! Stop!" she cried, "or I'll make complaints
to the great white throne and the ruling saints."

So the cowboy halted, I must confess,
And failed to bestow that fond caress.
Said he: "Miss Angel, it's shore too bad,
This sort of a country makes me sad,
Where there ain't no night, an' it's always day,
And the beautiful ladies won't even play.
Where there's wonderful houses and golden streets
But nobody sleeps and nobody eats.
Them beautiful rivers, it's sad to think,
There ain't no hosses nor cows to drink.
There's all this grass a-goin' to seed;
There ain't no critters to eat the feed.

A man can't gamble—there's so much gold
He could pick up more than his clothes would hold.
What's the use of the judge and the great white throne,
Where troubles and fights was never known?
I'm sorry, Miss, but I tell you true,
This ain't no place for a buckaroo."

Then she asked him about his former life;
She learned he had never possessed a wife.
But this angel lady, so sweet and nice,
Informed him that she had been married twice.
Her husbands had both been quiet men,
But she thought if she had it to do again
She'd have to decide between the two,
The sailor boy, or a buckaroo.
She seated herself upon his knees,
And gave his neck such a hearty squeeze,
Just then he heard an excited call,
'Twas a gray old saint on the city wall.
He flopped his robes and he waved his arm
Till a crowd had gathered in great alarm.
And then the cowboy stood alone
Before the judge, and the great white throne.

"What's this?" the judge of creation cried:
"How came this fellow to get inside?
Age must be dimming Saint Peter's eye
To let a spirit like that get by.
Just look at his face, with its desert brown,
And his bandy legs 'neath his angel gown.
He's a buckaroo, I know them well;
They don't even allow them into Hell!
He hasn't been here a half a day,
And he started an angel to go astray.
We can't permit him to stay at all,
Just pitch him over the outside wall."
So the saints and angels gave him a start,
And he went toward the earth like a falling dart.
But he never remembered the time he lit,
For he wakened before the tumble quit.
The winter wind blew cold and sharp
And the frost lay thick on the cowboy's tarp.

His beautiful vision had come to grief,
So he baked his biscuit and fried his beef.
And he drank some coffee, black and strong,
But all that day as he rode along
He thought of the saint who had butted in,
And he said to himself (with a wicked grin):
"I wish I had hold of that old saint chap,
I'd grab his whiskers and change his map.
I'd jump on his frame and stomp aroun'
Till I tromped him out of his saintly gown."

And all his life, as he roamed and toiled,
He thought of the vision so sadly spoiled.
The meddlesome saint that caused it all,
When he gave the alarm from the jasper wall.
He didn't repent, nor he didn't pray,
But he always wished they'd let him stay.

THE OLD NIGHT HAWK

BRUCE KISKADDON

I am up tonight in the pinnacles bold
Where the rim towers high,
Where the air is clear and the wind blows cold
And there's only the horses and I.
The valley swims like a silver sea
In the light of the big full moon,
And strong and clear there comes to me
The lilt of the first guard's tune.

The fire at camp is burning bright,
Cook's got more wood than he needs.
They'll be telling some windy tales tonight
Of races and big stampedes.
I'm gettin' too old fer that line of talk:
The desperaders they've knowed,
Their wonderful methods of handling stock,
And the fellers they've seen get throwed.

I guess I'm a dog that's had his day,
Though I still am quick and strong.
My hair and my beard have both turned gray
And I reckon I've lived too long.
None of 'em know me but that old cook, Ed,
And never a word he'll say.
My story will stick in his old gray head
Till the break of the Judgement Day.

What's that I see a walkin' fast?
It's a hoss a slippin' through.
He was tryin' to make it out through the pass;
Come mighty near doin' it too.
Git back there! What are you tryin' to do?
You hadn't a chance to bolt.
Old boy, I was wranglin' a bunch like you
Before you was even a colt.

It's later now. The guard has changed.
One voice is clear and strong.
He's singin' a tune of the old time range
I always did like that song.
It takes me back to when I was young
And the memories came through my head
Of the times I have heard that old song sung
By voices now long since dead.

I have traveled better than half my trail,
I am well down the further slope.
I have seen my dreams and ambitions fail,
And memory replaces hope.
It must be true, fer I've heard it said,
That only the good die young.
The tough old cusses like me and Ed
Must stay till the last dog's hung.

I used to shrink when I thought of the past
And some of the things I have known.
I took to drink, but now at last,
I'd far rather be alone.
It's strange how quick a night goes by,
Fer I live in the days of old.
Up here where there's only the hosses and I;
Up in the pinnacles bold.

The two short years that I ceased to roam,
And I led a contented life.
Then trouble came and I left my home,
And I never have heard of my wife.
The years that I spent in a prison cell
When I went by another name;
For life is a mixture of Heaven and Hell
To a feller that plays the game.

They'd better lay off of that wrangler kid;
They've give him about enough.
He looks like a pardner of mine once did,
He's the kind that a man can't bluff.
They'll find that they are making a big mistake
If they once git him overhet;
And they'll give him as good as an even break,
Or I'm takin' a hand, you bet.

Look, there in the East is the Mornin' Star,
It shines with a fiery glow
Till it looks like the end of a big cigar,
But it hasn't got far to go.
Just like the people that make a flash,
They don't stand much of a run,
Come bustin' in with a sweep and dash
When most of the work is done.

I can see the East is gettin' gray,
I'll gather the hosses soon,
And faint from the valley far away
Comes the drone of the last guard's tune.
Yes, life is just like the night-herd's song
As the long years come and go.
You start with a swing that is free and strong,
And finish up tired and slow.

I reckon the hosses all are here.
I can see that T-bar blue,
And the buckskin hoss with the one split ear;
I've got 'em all. Ninety two.
Just listen to how they roll the rocks
These sure are rough old trails.
But then, if they can't slide down on their hocks
They can coast along on their tails.

The wrangler kid is out with his rope,
He seldom misses a throw.
Will he make a cow hand? Well I hope,
If they give him half a show.
They are throwin' the rope corral around,
The hosses crowd in like sheep.
I reckon I'll swaller my breakfast down
And try to furgit and sleep.

Yes, I've lived my life and I've took a chance,
Regardless of law or vow.
I've played the game and I've had my dance,
And I'm payin' the fiddler now.

BOOMER JOHNSON

HENRY HERBERT KNIBBS

Now Mr. Boomer Johnson was a gettin' old in spots,
But you don't expect a bad man to go wrastlin' pans and pots;
But he'd done his share of killin' and his draw was gettin' slow,
So he quits a-punchin' cattle and he takes to punchin' dough.

Our foreman up and hires him, figurin' age had rode him tame,
But a snake don't get no sweeter just by changin' of its name.
Well, Old Boomer knowed his business – he could cook to
　　　make you smile,
But say, he wrangled fodder in a most peculiar style.

He never used no matches – left 'em layin' on the shelf,
Just some kerosene and cussin' and the kindlin' lit itself.
And, pardner, I'm allowin' it would give a man a jolt
To see him stir *frijoles* with the barrel of his Colt.

Now killin' folks and cookin' ain't so awful far apart,
That musta been why Boomer kept a-practicin' his art;
With the front sight of his pistol he would cut a pie-lid slick,
And he'd crimp her with the muzzle for to make
　　　the edges stick.

He built his doughnuts solid, and it sure would curl your hair
To see him plug a doughnut as he tossed it in the air.
He bored the holes plum center every time his pistol spoke,
Till the can was full of doughnuts and the shack was
　　　full of smoke.

We-all was gettin' jumpy, but he couldn't understand
Why his shootin' made us nervous when his cookin'
　　　was so grand.
He kept right on performin', and it weren't no big surprise
When he took to markin' tombstones on the covers of his pies.

They didn't taste no better and they didn't taste no worse,
But a-settin' at that table was like ridin' in a hearse;
You didn't do no talkin' and you took just what you got,
So we et till we was foundered just to keep from gettin' shot.

When at breakfast one bright mornin', I was feelin' kind of low,
Old Boomer passed the doughnuts and I tells him plenty: "No,
All I takes this trip is coffee, for my stomach is a wreck."
I could see the itch for killin' swell the wattles on his neck.

Scorn his grub? He strings some doughnuts on the muzzle of
       his gun,
And he shoves her in my gizzard and he says, "You're takin'
       one!"
He was set to start a graveyard, but for once he was mistook;
Me not wantin' any doughnuts, I just up and salts the cook.

Did they fire him? Listen, pardner, there was nothin' left to fire,
Just a row of smilin' faces and another cook to hire.
If he joined some other outfit and is cookin', what I mean,
It's where they ain't no matches and they don't need kerosene.

We have never before heard of a printed source for this particular verse which comes to us by way of Harry Taylor from Jackson Hole, Wyoming.

MURPH AND McCLOP

ANONYMOUS

It was a late afternoon in a cowtown saloon
At the end of a big rodeo,
And the boys from the chutes in their Levis and boots
Were wandering in to hash over the show.

The drinks were poured out with a roar and a shout
When a puncher hollered, "You bet."
Then a kid by the door sat down on the floor
And muttered, "How rank can you get."

When out of the gloom and into the room
Walked a maid with pain in her eyes.
The cowboys were stilled as though they'd been chilled,
So intense was their painful surprise.

For they all knew this lass and what had come to pass
When she married this wild buckaroo.
Their life had been brief, nothing but grief, and
Only lasted an hour or two.

The room was like death
and each man held his breath
Then she finally spoke
through the cigarette smoke.

"There's no need to fear, I want'cha to hear
Why my marriage turned out as a flop.
There's two men to blame and I'm willin' to name
None other than Murph and McClop.

"Now this gold wedding band that I have on my hand
Was a gift from a man I adore
Who solemnly said on the day we were wed
That he'd ride buckin' horses no more.

"As we drove through the night in the moon's silver light
He was mine, and my joyous heart sang.
For he said, 'I am through as a wild buckaroo
For I'm quitting the rodeo gang.

" 'Now, the rodeo life has no room for a wife
So I'll give up my riding for you.'
He said 'Go to hell' to the life he loved well
And I heard myself saying 'I do'."

Then they stopped rather short in a small auto court
To enjoy their first evening alone.
And she hastily dressed in the things she had best,
In the nicest silk things that she owned.

They were sweetly tucked in but a horrible din
Brought the romancin' straight to a stop,
When whom should appear with a giggle and lear
But none other than Murph and McClop.

"We just happened by when your car caught my eye,"
Said Murph with a devil-like smile.
"And because I'm your friend, I thought I'd offend
If I didn't drop by for awhile."

Then he took off his hat and stretched out on his back
And said "I'm weary with booze,
And I might take a snooze
If you'd offer me a space in your sack."

When up spoke McClop as he pulled off the top
Of a bottle of Mexican brew,
And he started to cry and sayin' goodbye
To the best bronco rider he'd knew.

Sayin', "Farewell, old friend, we have just seen the end
Of a trio beyond compare.
There's a big rodeo up in north Idaho
And we'd better get started for there."

"Then my darlin' jumps up and replenishes his cup
With a shot and a couple of beers,
And the boys gave accounts of jug-headed mounts
They'd drawn in the past seven years."

"Then my groom turned to me with a soul-searching plea."
Then her murmuring heart took a drop.
"I'll return by your side after one final ride.
But I'm going with Murph and McClop."

Now the lone evenin' star shone down on the bar
In this rodeo town in the West.
The air was a place of nothing but disgrace
And the cowboys were shorely depressed.

The woman was pale as she finished her tale.
She said, "Here's a toast to the source
To my brand-new divorce,
To none other than Murph and McClop."

Then Murph latched his seat to slow draggin' feet
To leave the scene of despair.
All followed behind. the guilty in mind,
While McClop led a down-trodden air.

In a soft dreary tone, more like a moan,
Came the little-eyed comment, "You bet."
While the kid by the door still remained on the floor
And muttered, "How rank can you get!"

This anonymous poem comes to us through a recitation by Waddie
Mitchell of Lee-Jigs, Nevada. Some say it is a Bruce Kiskaddon poem.

SILVER BELLS AND
GOLDEN SPURS

ANONYMOUS

'Twas a mining town called Golden Gulch
While the West was yet untamed.
There two bad men met, made a bet,
And the winnings never claimed.

The boys had ridden into town
One payday afternoon
To line the bar at the Lucky Star,
Which was Dandy Ran's saloon.

Now the dandy was an onry cuss
If by chance you made him sore,
His only law was the lightning draw
Of the heavy guns he wore.

On his watchchain hung a dozen bells
Of the finest silver spun,
Each tiny bell for a man that fell
When the dandy drew his gun.

They seemed to jingle merrily
To a tune that brought him luck,
But they rang the bell for the man that fell
When the dandy rang them up.

Well the boys had finished a round of drinks
When the bar room door swang wide,
And a man walked in with a reckless grin
And a funny cat-like stride.

On his dusty boots were golden spurs,
His face was lean and brown,
And at each hip the well-matched grips
Of six guns holstered down.

He spoke in a voice that was deathly quiet
And said, "I've come to waste some shells
On a man they say whose draw is quick
With a chain of silver bells.

"A dozen bells for a dozen men
Buried somewhere on the plain,
It's my intent to beat that gent,
I've come for the dandy's chain.

Well the dandy faced the stranger's gaze,
His coat was buttoned tight,
A gun swang free above each knee,
But the bells were hid from sight.

"So, it's the dandy's silver bells
On which your heart is set.
That's a fancy pair of spurs you wear,
Would you care to make a bet?

"The silver bells for the golden spurs,
But I'll warn you from the start.
You'll lose that bet and all you'll get
Is a bullet through the heart."

Well the stranger smiled his reckless grin
And said, "If the dandy tries
They'll find him dead with a chunk of lead
Placed neat between the eyes."

Then the stranger unbuckled his golden spurs
And slid them along the bar,
Said, "I'm callin' the hand of Dandy Ran,
Come out wherever you are."

Then slowly the dandy's hand went down
And unbuttoned his lapel,
And there it rest on checkered vest,
The chain of silver bells.

The stranger watched with narrowed eyes,
The time had passed for talk.
He hadn't drawed but his hands were clawed,
Like the feet of a diving hawk.

Then suddenly the dandy's hand went down
For his right-hand gun.
No one saw the stranger draw,
But two shots rang out as one.

The dandy stumbled to his knees
With a look of wild surprise, and
With a chunk of lead, like the stranger said,
Placed neat between the eyes.

The stranger stood at the end of the bar,
Apparently unhurt,
Except for a spot of red that slowly spread
Beneath the left pocket of his shirt.

The Golden Gulch is a ghost town now,
Its mining days are done.
There are coyote tracks in the tumbled shacks
Bleached white by the desert sun.

The Lucky Star is deserted, too,
All littered with sand and straw,
Where the laughter rang and the dandy's gang
Once drank to his lightning draw.

And the silver bells and the golden spurs
Still hang in their place of fame,
Above the bar at the Lucky Star
Still waiting the victor's claim.

This poem, with various titles, has been passed around among other western states with hellish features. This version was recited by Roy Green of Shandon, California.

HELL IN TEXAS

ANONYMOUS

The devil in Hades we're told was chained,
And there for a thousand years remained.
He did not grumble nor did he groan,
But determined to make a hell of his own
Where he could torture the souls of men
Without being chained in that poisoned pen.

So he asked the Lord if he had on hand
Anything left when he made the land.
The Lord said, "Yes, I have lots on hand,
But I left it down on the Rio Grand."

So the Devil went down and looked at the stuff,
And said if it comes as a gift he'd be stuck
For after examining it carefully and well,
He found it was too dry for hell.

So in order to get it off'n his hands
The Lord promised the Devil to water the land,
For he had some water, or rather some dregs,
That smelled just like a case of bad eggs.

So the deal was made and the deed was given
And the Lord went back to his home in heaven.
"Now," says the Devil, "I have all that's needed
To make a good Hell," and thus he succeeded.

He put thorns on the cactus and horns on the toads
And scattered tarantulas along the road.
He gave spiral springs to the bronco steed
And a thousand legs to the centipede.

And all will be mavericks unless they bore
Thorns and scratches and bites by the score.
The sand burrs prevail and so do the ants,
And those who sit down need half soles on their pants.

Oh, the wild boar roams the black chaparrel,
It's a hell of a place he's got for Hell.

The red pepper grows on the banks of the brooks,
The Mexicans use them in all that they cook.
Just dine with the Mexican, you'll be sure to shout
From Hell on the inside as well as the out.

Curley Fletcher's poems have the wild instincts of a desert bronc.

THE STRAWBERRY ROAN

CURLEY FLETCHER

I'm a-layin' around, just spendin' muh time,
Out of a job an' ain't holdin' a dime,
When a feller steps up, an' sez, "I suppose
That you're uh bronk fighter by the looks uh yure clothes."

"Yuh figures me right—I'm a good one," I claim,
"Do you happen tuh have any bad uns tuh tame?"
He sez he's got one, uh bad un tuh buck,
An' fur throwin' good riders, he's had lots uh luck.

He sez that this pony has never been rode,
That the boys that gets on 'im is bound tuh get throwed,
Well, I gets all excited an' asks what he pays
Tuh ride that old pony uh couple uh days.

He offers uh ten spot. Sez I, "I'm yure man,
Cause the bronk never lived, that I couldn't fan;
The hoss never lived, he never drew breath,
That I couldn't ride till he starved plum tuh death.

"I don't like tuh brag, but I got this tuh say,
That I ain't been piled fur many uh day."
Sez he, "Get yure saddle, I'll give yuh uh chance."
So I gets in his buckboard an' drifts tuh his ranch.

I stays until mornin', an' right after chuck
I steps out tuh see if that outlaw kin buck.
Down in the hoss corral, standin' alone,
Was this caballo,* uh strawberry roan.

His laigs is all spavined* an' he's got pigeon toes,
Little pig eyes an' uh big Roman nose,
Little pin ears that touch at the tip
An' uh double square iron stamped on his hip.

Ewe-necked an' old, with uh long lower jaw,
I kin see with one eye he's uh reg'lar outlaw.
I puts on muh spurs—I'm sure feelin' fine—
Turns up muh hat, an' picks up muh twine.

I throws that loop on 'im, an' well I knows then,
That before he gets rode I'll sure earn that ten,
I gets muh blinds on him, an' it sure was a fight,
Next comes muh saddle—I screws it down tight.

An' then I piles on 'im, an' raises the blind,
I'm right in his middle tuh see 'im unwind.
Well, he bows his old neck, an' I guess he unwound,
Fur he seems tuh quit livin' down on the ground.

He goes up t'ward the East, an' comes down t'ward the West,
Tuh stay in his middle, I'm doin' muh best.
He sure is frog walkin', he heaves uh big sigh,
He only lacks wings fur tuh be on the fly.

He turns his old belly right up toward the sun,
He sure is uh sun-fishin' son-of-uh-gun,
He is the worst bucker I seen on the range,
He kin turn on uh nickle an' give yuh some change.

While he's uh-buckin' he squeals like uh shoat,*
I tell yuh, that pony has sure got muh goat.
I claim that, no foolin', that bronk could sure step,
I'm still in muh saddle, uh-buildin' uh rep.

He hits on all fours, an' suns up his side,
I don't see how he keeps from sheddin' his hide.
I loses muh stirrups an' also muh hat,
I'm grabbin' the leather an' blind as uh bat.

With uh phenomenal jump he goes up on high
An' I'm settin' on nothin', way up in the sky,
An' then I turns over, I comes back tuh earth
An' lights in tuh cussin' the day of his birth.

Then I knows that the hosses I ain't able tuh ride
Is some of them livin'—they haven't all died.
But I bets all muh money they ain't no man alive
Kin stay with that bronk when he makes that high dive.

caballo Spanish for horse
spavined turned out feet because of swollen growths on a horse's legbones
shoat a young pig

THE FLYIN' OUTLAW

CURLEY FLETCHER

Come gather 'round me, cowboys,
And listen to me close
Whilst I tells yuh 'bout a mustang
That must uh been a ghost.

Yuh mighta heard of a cayuse,*
In the days they called 'em a steed,
Thet spent his time with the eagles
And only come down fer his feed.

He goes by the name of Pegasus,
He has himself wings to fly;
He eats and drinks in the Bad Lands,
And ranges around in the sky.

Seems he belongs to an outfit,
Some sisters, The Muses, they say,
And they always kep 'im in hobbles
Till he busts 'em and gets away.
Fer years they tries hard to ketch 'im,
But he keeps right on runnin' free;
The riders wore way too much clothes then,
Cowboys was knights then, yuh see.

He sure bears a bad reputation,
I don't sabe* how it begin,
Part eagle, part horse, and a devil;
They claims that he's meaner than sin.

I'm a-ridin' that rimrock country
Up there around Wild Horse Springs,
And I like to fell out uh my saddle
When that bronk sails in on his wings.

I feels like I must be plumb crazy,
As I gazes up over a bank,
A-watchin' that albino mustang
Uh preenin' his wings as he drank.

Finally he fills up with water.
Wings folded, he starts in to graze,
And I notice he's headin' up my way
Where I straddle my horse in a daze.

And then I comes to, all excited,
My hands is a-tremblin' in hope,
As I reaches down on my saddle
And fumbles a noose in my rope.

Ready, I rides right out at him
Spurrin' and swingin' my loop
Before he can turn and get going
I throws—and it fits like a hoop.

I jerks out the slack and I dallies,
I turn and my horse throws him neat,
And he lets out a blood curdlin' beller
While I'm at him hogtyin' his feet.

I puts my hackamore* on him,
And a pair uh blinds on his eyes;
I hobbles his wings tight together
So he can't go back to the skies.

I lets him up when he's saddled,
My cinch is sunk deep in his hide;
I takes the slack out uh my spur straps
'Cause it looks like a pretty tough ride.

I crawls him just like he was gentle,
I'm a little bit nervous, you bet;
I feels pretty sure I can ride 'im,
I still has his wings hobbled yet.

I raises the blinds and he's snortin',
Then moves like he's walkin' on eggs;
He grunts and explodes like a pistol;
I see he's at home on his legs.

Wolves, and panthers, and grizzlies,
Centipedes, triantlers, and such;
Scorpions, snakes, and bad whiskey
Compared to him wasn't much.

I got a deep seat in my saddle
And my spurs both bogged in the cinch;
I don't aim to take any chances,
I won't let him budge me an inch.

He acts like he's plumb full uh loco,
Just ain't got a lick uh sense;
He's weavin' and buckin' so crooked
That I thinks of an Arkansaw fence.

I'm ridin' my best and I'm busy
And troubled a-keepin' my seat;
He didn't need wings fer flyin',
He's handy enough on his feet.

He's got me half blind and I weaken,
He's buckin' around in big rings;
Besides which he kep me a-guessin',
A-duckin', and dodgin' his wings.

By golly he starts gettin' rougher,
He's spinnin' and sunfishin', too.
I grabs me both hands full uh leather;
I'm weary and wishin' he's through.

He hits on the ground with a twister
That broke the wing hobbles, right there;
Before I can let loose and quit him,
We're sailin' away in the air.

He smoothes out and keeps on a climbin'
Till away down, miles below,
I gets me a look at the mountains
And the peaks all covered with snow.

Up through the clouds, I'm a-freezin',
Plumb scared and I'm dizzy to boot;
I sure was a-wishin' I had me
That thing called a parachute.

And then I musta gone loco,
Or maybe I goes sound asleep,
'Cause when I wakes up I'm a-layin'
Right down on the ground in a heap.

He may uh had wings like an angel,
And he may uh been light on his feet,
But he oughta had horns like the devil
And a mouth fit fer eatin' raw meat.

I've lost a good saddle and bridle,
My rope and some other good things,
But I'm sure glad to be here to tell yuh
To stay off uh horses with wings.

cayuse an unruly, lazy, or wild horse
sabe or "savvy," from the Spanish *saber*, to know or understand
hackamore from the Spanish *jaquima*, a halter with reins, usually used with a
bosal (braided rawhide noose) rather than a bit

THE COWBOY'S PRAYER

CURLEY FLETCHER

Out on the western prairies,
While a-ridin' after stock,
A cowboy met a shepherd
A-tendin' to his flock.

The shepherd asked the cowboy
If he would like to stay
And join him in a little drink
And put some grub away.

The cowboy says, "That's good enough,
When my belly's full of stew
We'll bury the old tomahawk
And have a drink or two."

Now the herder cooked up quite a feed
And the cowboy ate his share.
Then the herder got the jug out,
And they started in from there.

"Let's have a drink," the cowboy says,
"We'll forget about our war,
Well, sure, let's have another one,
And then we'll have one more."

Back and forth they passed the jug
Until they went to sleep,
This puncher with the cattle and
The herder with the sheep.

Now the cowboy slept beneath the sage,
And he was awful tight.
He rolled and tumbled all about
And snored with all his might.

His arm fell over a tarrantula's hole,
This made the spider mad.
He sank his fangs into the arm
And gave it all he had.

The cowboy waked and sobered up,
His arm all swelled and black.
He awakened the shepherd
And they started for the shack.

The herder says, "That's pretty bad,
Looks like your Judgement Day.
If I was in your boots, cowboy,
I'd start right in to pray."

"I'd like to pray," the cowboy said,
"But I'm not quite sure just how,
So I'm gonna do the best I can
And I'd better start right now."

He braced hisself on bended knees,
And raisin' up his head
He cast his eyes toward Heaven,
And this is what he said:

"Lord, if you see this poor cowboy,
Come down and lend a hand,
Don't send your little son Jesus, Lord,
Boys sometimes don't understand.

"Now, Lord, I ain't one of them sinners
That's callin' on you right along,
I wouldn't be takin' your time up
Lest there was somethin' awful wrong.

"I'm a damn good bronc rider
And a ropin' son of a gun,
It's many an outlaw I've ridden,
And it's many a dollar I've won.

"I've always been good to my horses,
Till today I ain't never ate sheep.
I never did shirk on no round-up,
And I've always been worth my keep.

"I never did wrestle no cow,
I never took up with no squaw,
I never fought lest I had to,
And then I never went first on the draw.

"Course you know this better than I do,
But it don't seem hardly right
For me to be cashing my chips in
From some pot-bellied spider's bite.

"He crawled up while I was sleepin',
And he bit me while I was drunk.
I don't like to be belly-achin',
But now that was the trick of a skunk.

"If I was hurt while ridin' a bronco
Or ropin' a steer, Don't you see?
I wouldn't be here a beefin',
I'd figure it was comin' to me.

"I've lived by my creed as I saw it.
And all that I ask is what's fair,
And if you've been keepin' the cases
You know that I've been on the square."

Now this was the prayer of a cowboy,
The prayer that was frank and sincere,
'Cause he called on his God as he saw it,
To lend him a listenin' ear.

This cowboy's God must have heard him,
Out on the plains that day,
For he healed the suffering rider,
And he sent him upon his way.

This version of a cowboy's prayer, a common theme and mode of narration among cowboy poets, is one of the best known poems of Badger Clark, the revered South Dakota poet who wrote in the early part of the century.

A Cowboy's Prayer

BADGER CLARK

Oh Lord, I've never lived where churches grow.
    I love creation better as it stood
That day You finished it so long ago
    And looked upon Your work and called it good.
I know that others find You in the light
    That's sifted down through tinted window panes,
And yet I seem to feel You near tonight
    In this dim, quiet starlight on the plains.

I thank You, Lord, that I am placed so well,
    That You have made my freedom so complete;
That I'm no slave of whistle, clock or bell,
    Nor weak-eyed prisoner of wall and street.
Just let me live my life as I've begun
    And give me work that's open to the sky;
Make me a pardner of the wind and sun,
    And I won't ask a life that's soft or high.

Let me be easy on the man that's down;
    Let me be square and generous with all.
I'm careless sometimes, Lord, when I'm in town,
    But never let 'em say I'm mean or small!
Make me as big and open as the plains,
    As honest as the hoss between my knees,
Clean as the wind that blows behind the rains,
    Free as the hawk that circles down the breeze!

Forgive me, Lord, if sometimes I forget.
    You know about the reasons that are hid.
You understand the things that gall and fret;
    You know me better than my mother did.
Just keep an eye on all that's done and said,
    And right me, sometimes, when I turn aside,
And guide me on the long, dim, trail ahead
    That stretches upward toward the Great Divide.

Nyle A. Henderson breaks horses and recites poems out of his ranch in Hotchkiss, Colorado.

"BUENO," WHICH IN SPANISH MEANS GOOD

NYLE A. HENDERSON

Stick around now and I'll tell ya one more,
This happened to me, when I was with the Figure 4.
I'd been out doctorin' cows all afternoon,
And it was just about dark on the last day of June.

The day it seemed had gone awful slow,
I'd been workin' with a Mexican named Emelio.
He was fair with a rope and not too bad with a horse,
So our biggest problem was our language, of course.

I explained what we was doin' as best I could,
He just smiled and said, "Bueno," which in Spanish means
       good.
We found a lame cow down by the spring,
So I figured it was time that we do our thing.

I says to Emelio, "What would you say
If we doctor this cow and then call it a day?"
Now my horse was tired and needed a rest,
So I decided to put ol' Emelio to the test.

I told him to rope her and I hoped that he would.
He just smiled and said, "Bueno," which in Spanish
                    means good.
I circled around to run her out from the trees,
And she took off like a feather that's caught in a breeze.

And then there went Emelio on a dead run.
I just stood there and thought, now this might be fun.
She dove down through the brush like an old freight train,
Right behind her was Emelio, he didn't complain.

After awhile a yell came up out of the draw.
So I rode down to a clearing and guess what I saw?
He'd caught her and stopped and dallied up tight,
But you should have seen Emelio, man what a sight!

His shirt was all tore and he'd lost his hat.
He wasn't feelin' too happy, I'll bet you on that.
I was still laughin' 'bout the time that he'd had,
And then I saw that Emelio was gettin' kinda mad.

I gave her a shot so he could turn her loose,
Then Emelio decided it was time to cook my goose.
He undid his rope and that set her free,
She was plum on the fight and a-lookin' at me.

I beat it for the brush and I'm tellin' ya now,
I didn't want nothin' to do with that mean ol' cow.
I climbed as high as I could in an old oak tree,
And then I saw Emelio was a laughin' at me.

But he wouldn't come and chase her off like he should,
He just smiled and said, "Bueno," which in Spanish
                    means good.

It was after dark when Emelio drove that old cow away,
And it felt awful good to get down, I'll have to say.

I got back on my horse and we headed for home,
Down through the darkness where the cattle all roam.
Now I thought about it as we rode along,
Tryin' to figure out just what it was that went wrong.

And I'll bet by now the moral you've guessed:
He who laughs last, always laughs best!
Then I said somethin' I knew he understood,
I just smiled and said, "Bueno," which in Spanish means good.

How Many Cows?

NYLE A. HENDERSON

A fella from town stopped by the other day.
The talk that we had sorta went this-a-way.
He said, "I've got something that I'd like to ask you,
And if you know the answer, I'd like to know, too.

"I want to be a rancher and at prices today,
How many cows would I need to make my livin' pay?
Would a thousand cows be better than just one or two?
Do you have any advice on what I should do?"

"Now that's a tough question I'll tell you for sure,
Not one that can be solved with any one cure.
Machinery's sky high and so is the land,
And interest rates are more than anyone can stand.

"And there's imports and embargoes and all the like,
Remember now, as a rancher that you can't go on strike.
There's politicians, vegetarians and ecologists, too,
And a hundred government agencies tellin' you what to do.

"There's the cost of fuel and fences and labor and seed,
And tools and tires and water and feed.
There's always a horse needin' shod and veterinary bills,
I'm tellin' ya friend, ranchin' ain't all thrills!

"Startin' early in spring you'll be calvin' all night,
There's still feedin' to be done and the water's froze tight!
Insurance and utilities are always goin' up,
And remember, that wife of yours is about ready to pup.

"The whole cost of operating hasn't yet reached a peak,
While the price of beef is just pretty darn weak.
So here is the answer to this little test,
The man with the fewest is doin' the best.

"Only he's not makin' more, like you might guess,
The fact is, my friend, he's just losin' less!"

This Texas poem comes from Carlos Ashley's book, The Spotted Sow and Other Hill Country Ballads.

OL' EDGAR MARTIN

CARLOS ASHLEY

I seen Ol' Edgar Martin a-ridin' by jus now,
    He's goin' up to Walker's to get that bald-faced cow.
Funny feller—Edgar—sorter quiet and queer.
    Why, he's been ridin' by that way for nearly twenty year.

I knowed 'im when he's jest a kid a-livin' at his aunt's—
    A-wearin' long-tailed hickry shirts 'thout no boots
        ner pants;
Sorter shied from other kids—his folks wuz all that way—
    A-grazin' off from all the herd, jus like a maverick stray.

He growed up in these post oak hills, a-huntin' fox and coon—
    Hell, I can hear his 'ol houn now a-bayin' to the moon
While boy and dog come down this flat—there warn't much
        town here then—
    Yeh, Edgar had a world o' range to run them varmints in.

But my, this town has changed a sight—it ain't the same a-tall;
    They've put in City Water Works and built a City Hall.
And Edgar's changed a heap hisself—he ain't quite understood
    That all the things he's honin' for are gone—and gone
        for good.

I reckon Edgar's sixty-five—a little feeble too—
    He never took to no one trade—ain't much that
        he kin do.
So he jus rides aroun' all day—a sorter "livin' sigh" —
    A lost and homeless kinda look a-starin' from his eye.

He starts at daylight for the hills, when herds is comin' down,
    And helps the ranchers and the boys to punch their stuff
        through town.
He hangs aroun' the pens all day to watch 'em load the cars—
    And nights—I've seen 'im on his porch jus lookin'
        at the stars.

He's pickin' up a little stuff for Bigg's Meat Market now—
    Like goin' up to Walker's there to get that bald-faced cow.
I noticed when he passed jus now he didn't have no houn'—
    So guess I'd better saddle-up and help 'im into town.

Georgie Sicking works a ranch near Fallon, Nevada, but grew up cowboying in Arizona. She takes great pride in her skills as a top hand with cattle.

To Be a Top Hand

GEORGIE SICKING

When I was a kid and doing my best to
Learn the ways of our land,
I thought mistakes were never made by
A real top hand.

He never got into a storm with a horse,
He always knew
How a horse would react in any case
And just what to do.

He never let a cow outfigure him
And never missed a loop.
He always kept cattle under control
Like chickens in a coop.

He was never in the right place at the wrong
Time or in anybody's way.
For working cattle he just naturally knew
When to move and when to stay.

I just about broke my neck tryin'
To be and do
All those things a good cowboy just
Naturally knew.

One day while riding with a cowboy
I knew was one of the best,
For he had worked in that country for a long
Time, had taken and passed the test,

I was telling of my troubles, some
Bad mistakes I'd made,
That my dreams of being a top cowgirl
Were startin' to fade.

This cowboy looked at me and said
With a sort of smile,
"A sorry hand is in the way all the time,
A good one just once in awhile."

Since that day I've handled lots of cattle
And ridden many a mile,
and I figure I'm doin' my share if I get
In the way just once in awhile.

OLD TUFF

GEORGIE SICKING

Old Tuff was a catch dog
Used where manzanita and oak brush were thick.
We used him on wild cattle,
Some of their hides were slick.

The homeliest dog I ever saw,
With a crooked right fore leg,
With the furry face of an airedale
And colored like the yolk of an egg.

He wasn't ours but followed
A neighbor to our place one day.
We used him a year before we returned him,
The neighbor lived far away.

We couldn't wait to take him to the maverick country,
For we couldn't figure how
One small ugly yaller dog
Could catch and hold a cow.

We soon jumped a long-eared yearlin'
And headed for her at a lope,
Jumping rocks and dodging brush.
I had a loop built in my rope.

Old Tuff he saw the yearlin'
About the same time as us
And headed right in after her,
That nervy little cuss.

He ran her up a canyon
And across a low divide.
I figured that he'd lose her
When she hit the downhill side.

We hurried up to catch her,
Our ponies at a run,
But Tuff had grabbed an ear
And throwed her, the little son of a gun.

The heifer got up and
He held her still by an ear.
She was so busy battlin' Tuff
She let me ride up near.

I just put my rope on her head
And then we tied her down.
Put the F. C. brand on her hip,
Tuff was happy as a clown.

During the year we branded many mavericks
And I tried hard enough
To be the first to catch a maverick
But couldn't beat Old Tuff.

One day John came and took him,
For he had long ears to brand.
We thanked him for the use of Tuff,
A real brushhand.

Jon Bowerman runs a ranch near Fossil, Oregon, and writes poems about fabled rodeo times and the buckaroo life.

FOR JEFF

JON BOWERMAN

You followed rodeo from Calgary to El Paso,
Ridin' the broncs and the bulls,
Knew the hunger and pain before every win
Like the rest of those hard-riding fools.
You paid all the costs to be your own boss
And saw about all this big land.
Then you found the life of the buckaroo
Beats everything else in the end.

At four hundred a month, grub and a bunk,
Ridin' from morning till night
Through the wind and the snow and the forty below,
And sometimes you ask yourself why.
When there's jobs with more pay and a much shorter day
Workin' inside where it's warm,
You still chose the life of the buckaroo
Out there in the cold and the storm.

On a broncy cayuse that's just got no use
For that hull or the man on his back,
He's raisin' a fuss and kickin' up dust
And workin' at shedding his pack.
But you try and stay astraddle of that beat-up old saddle
And hope that the cinch doesn't bust,
'Cause it's part of the life of the buckaroo
And you'll weather the storm if you must.

The cows are plumb wild and easily riled
And they crash down the hills through the brush,
So you follow, too, as you shake out a loop
And try and keep up in the rush.
'Cause they're hard runnin' critters and wild-eyed
         bunch; quitters
And follow is all you can do.
But the risks are worthwhile for the buckaroo
If he thinks he might catch one or two.

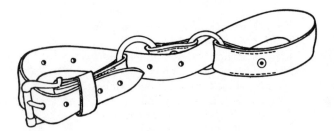

It's either too hot, or too cold when it's not,
But you're out every day just the same.
Glad you can be where the wind's blowin' free
With the smells of the wide open plain.
In this land that God saved for the juniper and sage
And critters and drifters like me,
He set it aside for the buckaroo,
Where everything's still wild and free.

cayuse disrespectful term for a horse, too wild or too tame. See "The Flyin'
Outlaw"

Tribute to Freckles and Tornado

JON BOWERMAN

There's a lot of tales in history about the American West,
Of the critters and the cowboys, the worst and the very best.
Broncs like Steamboat and Midnight, Descent and Prison Bars.
Cowboys like Mahan and Shoulders, just a few of the
        many stars.
But maybe never such a match-up as at that
        National Finals show
When Freckles Brown drew up on the bull they called Tornado.

Now two hundred and twenty cowboys had drawed
        that bull before,
But every one heard the whistle from the dirt of the
        arena floor.
And for all the many riders that had straddled that
        twistin' hide,

It was a short walk back to the chutes, 'cause they
            hadn't gone far in the ride.
Like an Oklahoma twister, he had the strength to
            move a barn,
And many felt that the cowboy that could ride him had
            not been born.

Now Freckles Brown was no youngster at the age of forty-six.
He'd been battered and bruised and broken and taken some
            awful licks.
But he'd also been the champion and as he warmed his
            rosin up,
He leaned on his years of experience, and maybe a little luck.
He took his final wrap and didn't hesitate,
Slid up on his rope and nodded for the gate.

An explosion of bull and cowboy seemed to fill the air!
Tornado turned back and twisted, but Freckles
            stuck right there.
With his left knee cocked to take the shock and his right spur
            clinching tight,
The cowboy hustled and scrambled, while the bull started
            spinning right.
Now a right turn was the cowboy's weak side, though you
            wouldn't think a bull would know,
But after about four seconds he had Freckles off his rope.

With each new jump it looked as though the bull
            had surely won,
But the cowboy kept on hustlin' and somehow hangin' on.
'Cause Freckles Brown had never learned the meaning of "quit."
Do or die was his way of life and he had a ride to fit.
Though slipping deeper into the well he still refused to fall,
And that screamin' crowd went wild as bull and cowboy gave
            their all.

Another spin but tighter yet as Freckles threw his
                free hand up,
And that tighter turn and scrambling luck put the
                cowboy back on top.
Now that twistin' terror Tornado was just a blur of
                white and red,
But the cowboy knew he had him beat and he drove his
                spurs ahead.
He couldn't hear the buzzer, above that screamin' din,
But he knew the time was finally up 'cause the clown came
                runnin' in.

For five more minutes that finals crowd screamed and cheered
                and roared.
'Cause someone had finally rode the bull that couldn't
                be rode before.
And though he may have cracked a grin as he walked back to
                the chutes,
Freckles' only comment was, "The bull was overdue."
But somewhere in the pages of history where they write
                such tales down,
There's the story of the bull Tornado, and the cowboy,
                Freckles Brown.

LAMBERT

GREY'S RIVER ROUNDUP

HOWARD NORSKOG

There's wonderful things in this world to do,
Like churches, home-living, and sin.
But I'd like to be back with Old Joker,
Ridin' the river again.

Papoose was in foal, Black Lady was gone,
I was breaking Old Joker to ride.
A sharp little bay from the Hoback,
Bred on the Jewitt side.

There are people without this idea,
And I know there are others of course,
But for me I love to be mounted
Astride of a Jewitt horse.

Dean fixed me up with Old Joker
After Blue Lady went home,
And the miles I rode on him and Papoose,
It's never being alone.

People are liars and sneak-thieves,
You don't know where the cheatin' begins,
But all of my problems diminish
Ridin' the river again.

Where the Grey's River cattle are feeding at
The roundup with Lloyd McNeil,
Each year when we left the Star Valley
In the early morning I'd feel

The shock of the cold that woke me up,
The beautiful world I was in,
Back on Old Joker at sunrise
Ridin' the river again.

Waddie Mitchell is one of the finest young reciters in the buckaroo tradition. He is ranch boss on a spread between Lee and Jiggs, Nevada.

THE BOOK

WADDIE MITCHELL

Not so awful long ago,
    Afore I married Toot
An' settled down an' had some kids,
    I wore a fancy boot.
An' rode with the big outfits
    Thet pulled the wagon out,
An' ropin' cows an' ridin' broncs
    Was all I cared about.

But even then the winters came,
    An' then a buckaroo
Would have to hunt him up a job
    To spend the winter through.
An' so I took a line camp,
    'Twas better then feedin' hay,
An' that's kinda where my story starts,
    On a cold December day.

We're camped there over two months now
    With nary time to play,
Aridin' fence an' spreadin' salt
    An' watchin' cows don't stray.
An' I'm feelin' purty sorry
    For this feller known as me,
Cuz I'm out here an' town's in there
    An' that's abotherin' me.

Stub gets up an' starts a fire and
    Rubs his frost-bit toes.
"The only place we'll sweat today
    Is underneath the nose."
It's the twenty-fifth day of December,
    The thermometer shows ten below.
The wind is blow'n from the north,
    The clouds are threatenin' snow.

I pulls out of my bedroll
    An' dresses to fight the cold.
Stub steps out to use the outhouse
    An' I thinks to m'self "how bold."
I goes down an' grains the horses,
    Chops the ice an' then some wood,
And when I gets back to the cabin
    Stub's got breakfast smellin' good.

We sit down to biscuits an' gravy,
    Venison steaks . . . black hot brew.
Not too much conversation
    Could be heard between us two.
I had reached the age of twenty-one
    An' was a wild buckaroo,
Stub couldn't have realized how I felt,
    Bein' an old man of forty-two.

"It just ain't fair I'm stuck out here,"
    I finally up and say.
"I should be in ol' Elko town
    Learnin' girlies how to play.
Celebratin' Christmas proper.
    Like them city people do,
Instead of bein' way out here
    With no one else but you."

A grin come over his snow-burnt face
    As he takes a sip of brew,
"If you'll let'm, Old Grandpa here
    Might say a word or two.
"I know this here is Christmas
    An' you feel you have no chance
To celebrate it proper
    Or attend the Christmas dance.

This ain't my first line-camp job,
    But I remember how it felt
The first time thet I just had beans
    'Stead'a a turkey 'neath my belt.
An' how no family nor friends were there
    To celebrate the day,
To drink the whiskey, exchange the gifts,
    An' while the hours away.

"But then I got to thinkin'
    This an' I asked myself right out,
Is this the way we celebrate the day
    What Christmas is all about?
An' I concluded that although it's merry
    To laugh an' exchange gifts an' such,
If we don't give as much time to the Savior
    The day hasn't gained us too much."

Now I didn't think Stub was a heathen,
    But I'd never heard him talk like that,
As if he was religious
    Or believed in stuff like that.
I probably look'd kind'er silly,
    Cuz it took me by surprise,
A him a talkin' out like that.
    He could see it in my eyes.

He said, "What's the matter?
    Don't you believe the Good Book's true?"
I said "I never give it much thought . . .
    Why? . . . Do you?"
"Well, I have some trouble read'n it
    The way them fellers write,
But it makes me feel real good inside,
    Like I'm doin' somethin' right.

"An' anyone in our occupation,
    See'n the things that cowboys see,
He knows there's a whole lot more out there,
    Somethin' much bigger than he,
Providin' water an' grasses,
    Mountains an' trees an' air,
A place for a calf to grow big an' fat
    An' a reason for man to be there.

"And the way I got it figured,
    Celebratin' Christmas should be two-fold.
Part for family, gifts an' friends,
    An' part for the Book of Old.
An' time to give thanks for the Savior,
    An' to rejoice at His Birth.
That He came and He made it possible
    For life for us after Earth.

"An seein' as how it's just you an' me
    An' the beans an' the coffee stout,
Well, the family an' friends,
    An' the turkey an' trims, we'll just have to do without.
But as far as celebratin' the day of the birth
    Of the Attonin' One,
I think it proper thet you an' me
    Set an' read on the Bible some."

So after the daily duties was done
    An' the beans was in the pot,
We sat 'n read us some of the Book
    (I don't remember jist what).
But it had to do with the birth of the Lord,
    Some wise men an' shepherds an' such,
An' I've heard the story a number of times since
    But I never enjoyed it so much.
But that day, as now an' always,
    Not just to be the man's dub,
It made me feel real good inside
    An' I'll always thank you for that . . . Stub.

THE THROW-BACK

WADDIE MITCHELL

'Twas the end of the nineteenth century
    When the cowboy era peak'd,
An' a motley clan of horse-back men
    Perfected a technique
Of handlin' an movin' cattle,
    A type raised primarily for meat,
Thus insurin' a hungry young nation
    There would always be plenty to eat.

But this entailed a great deal more
    Than most people are led to believe,
For in that time an' circumstance
    Nine hundred miles was hard to conceive.

But that's what they were up against
    With this long horn'd bovine beast,
For the product was in the expanse of the West
    And the market was in the East.

Now the problem was gettin' the product to market
    At a price all parties could pay,
So unlike Europe, where only royalty ate meat,
    The common man could have beef everyday.

But the obstacles seem'd near insurmountable,
    For the miles in between were not kind.
There were rivers to swim an' deserts to cross,
    An' water and forage to find
To keep the animals strong and healthy
    So they could walk twenty miles a day,
An' get to the railway before the snow flew
    To be loaded and shipped on their way.

Now to do this they'd have to be able
   To hire a man who would sleep on the ground
For seven long months out of one given year
   For forty a month, and found.

He'd have to own a few necessities,
   Like a saddle that cost at least two month's pay,
A bridle, a bedroll, a slicker, some chaps,
   Some spurs an' a mouth harp to play.

He'd have to accept varied menus,
   Like biscuits an' beans an' meat,
Or Meat an' beans an' biscuits
   With coffee throw'd in for a treat.

He'd have to enjoy the great outdoors,
   Cause that's where he'd be night an' day,
Except for the time he'd be behind bars
   In some little town 'long the way.

He'd have to be a high-skilled technician,
   Fulfill his job atop a low-bred feen,
Leave camp in the morn, make it back in at night,
   An' get somethin' done in between.

He'd have to savvy the ropes and
   Be proficient with his lariat skill,
For the man who can't handle this basic job,
   His worth to the outfit is nil.

Now you'd think with this list of requirements
   That the job would've been hard to fill,
But the human race now an' then breeds a throw-back,
   And for some reason these men fit the bill.

So through the years cowboys managed
   To keep beef in the stores to be bought,
An' the job requirements have changed some
   'Cause our country has grown up a lot.

Oh, we still have some of their problems,
    Mother Nature still kicks at our rumps.
The job will never be conducive to comfort,
    But you learn not to notice the bumps.

But now days they've throw'd us some ringers,
    New problems that's kick'd in our slats,
Like computers, the futures and unions,
    And worst of all . . . bureaucrats.

And the human race still breeds a throw-back,
    From their predecessor's mold they are pour'd,
And they're still puttin' beef in the market
    That the common man can afford.

But I can't see that lastin' forever,
    For we keep gettin' kick'd in the teeth,
An' if you don't think you're gettin' a bargain, Pard,
    Just go abroad an' order some beef.

ONE RED ROSE

ERNIE FANNING

I went into town one night
And when I got tired of walkin'
I stopped in this place to get a cup of coffee,
And I heard some young men talkin'.

They talked of the places they had been,
And the things that they had done.
I think they named most every trade,
That is, all except one,

And nowhere in their conversation
Did I ever chance to hear
One of them mention an outlaw horse,
Or a wild old bald-faced steer.

Now as I set and listened
I kinda got the hunch
That I might be one of the last
Of that old wild bunch.

And I thanked the Lord
That He was so good to me,
For I've had a chance to see and do
Things my grandkids will never see.

I've seen 5,000 head of steers
Stretch for miles and miles,
And when the storm clouds pass on over,
I've seen the punchers' faces break into smiles.

I've been dog-tired and dirty,
With my butt just fairly draggin',
Then someone'd say, "That's the last one, boys,"
And we'd head for the old chuck wagon.

Now Cookie was an old time kind of puncher,
He was rawhide tough and hard,
And he owned the ground around that wagon
For about two hundred yards.

And I can still hear
Old Cookie shout,
"Get that horse out of my kitchen
Or I'll brain you, there's no doubt,

"Out with them bat wings* and chihuahuas*
'Fore you come through my kitchen door,
I got enough dust around this wagon
Without you making any more."

An iffen you were smart,
You'd kinda heed old Cook
Or he'd wrap you round the horns
With an old gaunch hook.

Or just watch a bunch of mustangs
When they leave a water hole,
Or set on the edge of a crick
With an old skillet and pan for gold.

I've thought about when my ridin' is through,
And thinkin' of it isn't any fun,
But while we're on the subject,
Let me tell you how I want it done.

I want cowboys to carry my coffin
In Levis and a sweat-stained shirt.
And if there's no objection, I'd like
Their faces covered with dirt.

And for my funeral march
Play "Utah Carol" or one of those,
And I don't want no wiltin' flowers on my grave;
Cowboy, all I want's just one red rose.

And I guess my fondest wish,
I really shouldn't tell,
But I pray to God that when I die
I'll go right square to hell.

For it'd kinda be like punchin' cows
On the Arizona desert once more,
So goddamn hot at midnight
You can't touch a latch on the bunkhouse door.

They'd be horses there from the ol' RO's
And cows that carry the hook seven,
And I'm here to tell you people,
That stock could never get into heaven.

bat wings chaps, wide-winged for easy putting on and taking off
chihuahuas Mexican-style spurs

THE VANISHING VALLEY

ERNIE FANNING

Out on a Nevada mountain
While lookin' for his stock,
A cowboy stopped to rest his horse
A-top a big rimrock.

And as he set and looked
At the valley floor below,
He asked himself this question:
Where the hell did the valley go?

Whatever happened to the fields of spuds
And onions that the old degos used to raise,
And where have gone the lush green meadows
Where the fat cattle used to graze?

For as he set and looked down
Through the smog in the shimmering summer's heat,
What filled his vision most
Were mounds of steel and gray concrete.

And he knew there was no way to slow,
Much less halt,
The spreading of the buildings
And the ribbons of asphalt.

He could still remember when every man
In the valley helped pull his neighbor's load,
When Kietzke Lane was nothing more
Than a gravel country road,

When they drove fat cattle from the Humphrey lots
to the shippin' pens at Stanford Way.
Oh yeah, Cowboy,
But that was yesterday.

Well the cowboy stepped across his horse
And he started to the valley floor below,
And once more he asked himself a question:
Why the hell did this valley have to go?

Jesse Smith is a California cowboy.

SATURDAY NIGHT
IN WOODY

JESSE SMITH

It was late afternoon in the Woody Saloon
Over there on the west side of town.
Me and the boys were makin' some noise
And washin the branding dust down.

There was big Jim and me from the Old Flying Three
And some guys from the double OU.
There was two or three from the Triple IV
And some from the Double Horse Shoe.

We had all hit town about the same time, and
We had six month's pay in our polk.
It was easy to say that before the end of our stay
We'd all leave for the ranches plum broke.

There was two or three gals we considered our pals,
All them were ugly as sin.
But to us son-of-a-guns a-lookin' for fun
It didn't much matter right then.

Well the juke box was playing as loud as it could
By the time darkness came round
We were dancin' and yellin' as loud as we could,
You could hear us all over town.

Now the gals that had been so ugly before,
Why they was plum pretty by now,
And the faster we danced on into the night
The prettier they got somehow.

By midnight I'd say they was all beauty queens,
    With figures and faces to match.
"A man would be proud," I said right out loud,
    "If one of you beauties he'd catch."

Along about three my eyes couldn't see
    And my legs they weren't workin' too good.
Big Jim says to me, "We'd better leave,"
    And I says to Jim, "Yah, we should."

So we saddled up and we struck out at a lope,
    With my head a-poundin' real bad.
My pockets were empty, as you may have guessed,
    But look what a good time I had.

Well in five or six months I'll meet with the bunch
    Again at the Woody Saloon.
We'll spend all our cash but we'll have a big bash,
    Next fall when we bark at the moon.

SADDLE TRAMP

BUCK WILKERSON

Trail dust settled behind him,
Stirred up by the horse that he rode.
He was headin' back to a line camp
That was his temporary abode.

He had set in his saddle since sunup,
Pushing strays back toward the herd.
His horse was trained for that purpose
And he'd scarcely spoken a word.

He was an old cow puncher
Who wore the hair of a goat
To cover his legs from western storms,
And he wore a cowhide coat.

He wore Levis, boots and a Stetson,
That describes his attire (just about),
In the front of his shirt was a pocket
With a Bull Durham tag hangin' out.

From one outfit to another
He drifted with six in his string.
He lived the life of a loner
Just doin' his own thing.

He rode the unfenced ranges
In the wind and the rain and the sleet.
'Twas a toss-up which was more cruel,
That or the summer's heat.

Fifty a month was his wages,
That wasn't much – he'd confess,
But that bought his clothes and his makin's
And that's all he needed, I guess.

There was always a little left over
He'd save to spend in the joints,
To cut the dust from his tonsils
When he'd trail into shipping points.

This ode is set down in his memory;
He was one hell of a man in his day.
He has vanished – he's no longer needed,
His breed has just faded away.

Never again will you see him
Alone far out on the plains,
For now they use trucks to move cattle
And they count them from aeroplanes.

Don't try to follow the hoof prints,
You'd find them too dim, I'm afraid.
Nothing is left but the legend
Of the trail that the saddle tramp made.

Bob Schild is a respected saddle maker from Blackfoot, Idaho, and has cowboyed and rodeoed for years.

THE KID SOLOS

BOB SCHILD

Me, the kid, and some other boys was playin' a hand of cards,
Bent only on quiet pleasures and the company of our pards.
Thru all the blissful afternoon the aces came and went,
When our drinkin' was bare begun our money was
                mostly spent.

For an hour or two we worked on the brew, losses to forget.
The liquor it worked and up we perked when the kid made a
                wild bet.
He rose full of brew, he spoke to the crew, "Boys, now place
                your dough.
I'll fly from the window on the north and back by the
                west I'll go.

"You've won my gold, if I may be bold, by the turning
                of the card.
Now I'll take it back, and round this shack I'll solo these
                few yards."
Over his shoulders draped a sheet, then he leaped from the
                window's edge.
Down below I saw him go to crumple a barberry hedge.

The sirens wailed when the Doc we hailed, and they carried
      the kid away.
The hospital door I entered at four, my respects to pay.
Never had I seen a face so scratched or a body so broken up.
The kid just gazed, he looked half dazed, like a lonely
      spotted pup.

"By the Lord of the land, Pard, why'd you stand, seeing what
      I'd do?"
"I'm sorry, Kid, for what I did, but I lost ten on you too."

TWO OF A KIND

BOB SCHILD

The town was aflutter on rodeo week,
With bronc stompers there that were well past their peak.
The small western valley seemed fairly to glow
As time fast approached for the Old Timer's Show.

The hands that arrived there would fit the same mold;
Their features were weathered and faces looked old,
But one showed time's ravages more than the rest,
And hid not his blemishes though he tried his best.

A wrinkled old timer, his boot heels run down,
Blended quite well with the rest of the town.
A waxed cultured mustache adorned his thin lips
And two well-tended curls perched out on its tips.

I stood there transfixed by his look as he passed;
Like a gaunt war prisoner who once had been gassed.
He carried a look of near death in his eye.
My heart filled with pity as he hobbled by.

The crusty old cowboys were payin' their fees
With visions of bringing the world to its knees.
The weren't only bent on just makin' a dime,
But intended, also, to have a good time.

But then, to the window with faltering step,
Came that gnarled old twister to build up his rep.
I often remember the look in his eye
As he forked out the cash and paid for his try.

I felt overwhelmed by a strange sense of doom,
But try as I did I could not leave that room.
I watched while the old twister drew from the hat,
His true equal in age, the great Alley Cat.

His Fame was no fable, we'd all heard of that,
This vicious old outlaw, by name, Alley Cat;
He matched the old cowboy for wrinkles and groans.
I still had that feeling of doom in my bones.

The rest of the cowboys were sharing their fun;
The old twist and Alley Cat were having none.
They each faced the other and gazed through the fence;
Huge black clouds rolled in and the air grew so dense.

The time now had come for their effort to make;
Lightning was flashing, the earth was a lake.
The Alley Cat's age left a sway in his back;
A nigh perfect fit for such a badly-worn tack.

The old rider eased himself into the boat.
The arena out front filled up like a moat.
When Alley Cat broke, with a mighty high dive,
The wrinkled old twister did more than survive.

With no sign of age now observed in their fight,
'Twas plain that the ride would be high for the night.
The Alley Cat showed us the strength of his youth;
The twister was smiling, 'tis heaven's own truth.

The buckaroo hooking from maneline* to board
An Alley Cat pitching the highest that's scored;
But all of the rain and the mud that we had
Would make even sure-footed horses slip bad.

Old Alley Cat's age had long taken its toll.
He fell with a crash in a slippery mud hole,
And when we observed the results of the wreck,
We found Alley Cat dead, he'd fractured his neck.

The old twister quivered down there in the muck,
And as the sayin' goes he'd just run out of luck.
Pinned in the fracas an' damned by the flood
He'd never cut loose and was drowned in the mud.

They buried the two just the way they had gone,
Old cowboy aboard an' his saddle strapped on,
The Alley Cat making a twenty-four kick,*
The old timer, still smiling, showing his lick.

When crossing the rim rocks on weather's worst nights
The cries of the dead fuel immortal weird sights;
Mad visions of trail herds, wild horses and such,
Rise vaporlike into the heavens they touch.

Quite often, in moonlight, a ghost ride is seen,
It's flashed on the clouds like a TV machine;
And sometimes, by starlight, two lovers entwine,
Most always this feeling is pleasant and fine.

Sometimes I'm deluged by the strange sense of doom
I felt long ago while I stood in that room;
It's always with this that the lightning will flash,
Black clouds rumble in and the thunder will crash.

Then the old timer will strap on his saddle,
And there, in the clouds, once again they will battle;
The rain and the mud that precluded their plight
Comes urging them back to their tomb in the night.

maneline the top of the neck where the mane grows
twenty-four kick twenty-five is a perfect bronc kick in rodeo, although twenty is about as high a score as is ever given

Jim Hofer is from the Columbia River borderlands of Oregon and Washington. His lyrics are impressions from his years of shipping cattle by truck.

MATCHING GREEN RIBBON

JIM HOFER

She drove a green and black Mack,
It was a seven-axle doubles rig.
She had a matching green ribbon in her hair
And when she jammed them gears,
Well, that Mack it danced a jig.
And I loved her from that first moment there.

The next time I saw her the snow was flying cold,
We was high in the Rockies so bare.
I pulled up along side her
And I decided I'd be bold,
For I'd loved her from that first moment there.

Then it was in the Flinthills just south of Wichita,
We was loading some cattle out there.
As I looked around those grass hills
She was the finest thing I saw.
And I'd loved her from that first moment there.

And I saw her again in the driving rain
Out in west Texas somewhere.
The wet desert is so lonesome
I talked without shame,
For I'd loved her from that first moment there.

I loved her once more on a high prairie night,
Breathing that cool Alberta air.
I spoke to her so softly,
And loved her with all my might,
For I'd loved her from that first moment there.

Yes, she drove a green and black Mack,
A seven-axle doubles rig,
She wore a matching green ribbon in her hair
(Oh, that raven hair)
And when she jammed them gears,
Well, that Mack
It fairly-well thee danced a jig,
And I loved her from that first moment there.

Baxter Black may be the world's only full-time cowboy poet. His poems appear in a regular syndicated column, and he has published several books of cowboy poetry. He also tours extensively, reciting poems and stories all over the country.

A TIME TO STAY, A TIME TO GO

BAXTER BLACK

Ya know, I got this ranch from my daddy,
He come here in seventeen.
He carved this place outta muscle and blood;
His own and his ol' 'percheon team.*

I took over in fifty
And married my darlin' in May.
Together we weathered whatever came up.
She had what it took to stay.

Last winter we finally decided
We'd pack up and leave in the spring.
The kids are all grown and city-folk now;
We never raised 'em to cling.

Oh sure, I wished they'd have wanted
To ranch and carry it on,
But they did their part, I thank 'em fer that,
And they chose. Now all of 'ems gone.

The last thirty odd years we've collected
An amazing number of things!
Bonnets and bottles, clippings and letters,
And Dad's ol' surcingle rings.*

We've spent the winter months sorting.
Our hearts would ache or would jump
As we looked at our lives in trinkets we'd saved,
Then boxed up or took to the dump.

We cried sometimes in the attic,
I'm not ashamed of the truth.
I love this ol' ranch that we're leavin',
We gave it the strength of our youth.

I love this ol' woman beside me,
She held me and stayed by my side.
When I told 'er I's thinkin' 'bout sellin'
She said, "Honey, I'm here for the ride."

These new fellers movin' in Monday
Are nice and I wish 'em good luck.
But I'd rather be gone, so Ma, get yer stuff,
I've already gassed up the truck.

Lookin' back over my shoulder
At the mailbox, I guess that I know
There's a time to be stayin', a time to be goin',
And I reckon it's time that we go.

percheon team correctly spelled Percheron, a large English draft breed of
grey or black horses.
surcingle rings rings to which the girth strap cinches

L.E. Wallis

THE BIG HIGH AND LONESOME

BAXTER BLACK

The big high and lonesome's a place in my mind,
　　like out from Lakeview to Burns,
Or up on the Judith, or at Promontory
　　'bout where the U P track turns.
It's anywhere you feel tiny
　　when you get a good look at the sky,
And sometime's when it's a-stormin'
　　you can look the Lord in the eye.

I stood and watched in amazement
　　out on San Augustine Plain
While the sky turned as black as the curtains in Hell
　　and the wind come a-chasin' the rain.
And standing there watching I felt it
　　in the minutes before it arrived,
An unearthly stillness prickled my skin
　　like the storm itself was alive.

When it hit, it hit with a fury.
　　The wind with its sabre unsheathed
Led the charge with the scream of a demon,
　　the storm was barin' its teeth.
The thunder cracked and the sky split apart
　　with a horrible deafening roar.
I felt like a fox in a cage made of bones
　　in sight of the hounds at the door.

The blackness shook like a she-bear,
　　the lightning blinded the sun.
The rain fell like bullets around me,
　　scattering dust like a gun.
It was over as quick as it started,
　　leaving it peaceful instead.

The only sound was the beat of my heart
    pounding inside of my head.

I took off my hat too shaken to move,
    afraid of making a sound.
I felt like a man on the head of a pin
    with nobody else around.
But the sun was already sparkling
    in raindrops still wet on my face.
The big high and lonesome is only God's way
    of putting a man in his place.

---

*This poem is about the 1985 gathering of cowboy poets in Elko,
Nevada. Charley Kortes is a Wyoming rancher, and this poem appeared
in* Western Horseman.

POETS GATHERING, 1985

CHARLES A. KORTES

When the cowboy poets gathered it was nineteen eighty-five.
Cannon chose the town of Elko where cowboys still survive.
He and Big Jim Griffith, Meg Glaser, and their crew
Worked out a perfect program, and stayed to see it through.

The poets came from everywhere, especially states around.
All were pleased and happy with the many friends they found.
They told stories, quoted poems, several sang, and many read.
Others came to sit and listen, and write down what was said.

There were poems about the prairie, open spaces and the sky.
Rustlers, ranchers, Indians, and how cowboys live and die.
Songs were sung of the early West. when all was wild and free,
Of herding spooky cattle, or a cowhand on a spree.

Rodeo cowboys quoted poems, and told some stories too,
Of cowboy life right from the chute, and everything they knew.
Some poets felt uneasy when their name was called to quote,
And found their knees a-shakin', reading what they'd wrote.

All the poets had their say, and read what they had brought,
Singers had a chance to sing, and cowboys what they thought.
There never was a moment anyone could say was dull.
Things of interest all the time and every session full.

Hal Cannon and Jim Griffith, Meg Glaser and their crew
Conceived the poets gathering and they started something new,
Recording cowboy poems, old stories brought alive,
And all the many new ones heard, in nineteen eighty-five.

This and other poems by Nick Johnson were published in his book entitled Wind River Poems.

GREASIN' THE MILES

NICK JOHNSON

When night comes slippin' up the valley
And you've quite a ways to go,
And you just can't say for certain
Whether you'll make her in or no—
Oh, it ain't no use comparin'
Your snug cabin or your bed
To a bivouac near a windfall
With your saddle 'neath your head.

No use wishin' for the taters
Or the beefsteak that you'd get,
Nor comparin' them with water
And a homemade cigarette.
But just lift your head a trifle;
Try to sing some darn fool song,
And it's really quite surprisin'
How you'll grease the miles along.

And your pony, say, he'll get it
And start pullin' on the bit
Just to let you know he's with you
And still feelin' pert and fit,
And remember God Almighty's
Been about a million years
A pointin' us back to Eden
Through this sinsunk Vale of Tears.

And he's taught the grass and flowers
And the trees and waters, too,
How to laugh and sing and burble;
Come on stockhand, why can't you?
Cause we've got to learn to do it
'Fore we reach the millennium.
Me—I've done some heavy figurin',
If you're ready, here's the sum:

He give to Nature the winter
So she could recuperate;
And the night he give to us folks
To forget our pains and hate.
So if we learn to all be joyful,
"Just the way we like her, see,"
Why the trail will be lots shorter
And the quicker we'll be free.

NICK JOHNSON

We were camped just under Hawk's Rest,
Me and Al and a span of Dudes,
A lawyer out of Boston
And a Doc from Baton Rouge,
And they talked on vital subjects
Just the way them waddies* will
On how to love a woman
And the way to run a still.

In the west the sun was huntin'
For a place to roll his bed,
And he had his blankets scattered
Pink and brown and orange and red
In a heap of gay profusion
Clean across the western sky,
And the little stars came peeping out
As the light began to die.

You could hear the horse bells tinkle
In the park above our camp.
And the wind came up the valley
Blowing soft and smelling damp,
And it made the campfire flicker
As it rustled thru the wood,
Mixed the odor of the flowers
With the smell of cooking food.

Then the moon sent out a detail
For to scout among the peaks.
And they fetched the shadows jumpin'
In and out like hide-and-seek.
In the east a fox was barkin'

Out derision at the moon,
A followin' up his patrol.
Rosy red, shaped like a plume.

And the Doc turned to the lawyer
And he says, "God, ain't this dead;
Nothin' to do but sit and fidget,
Guess I'll chase myself to bed.
You can talk about Dame Nature,
But the next time that I go
For to see this wide and woolly West
I'll bring a radio."

waddies common cowboys

Linda Ash is from Trail, Oregon.

BELLERIN' AND BAWLIN'

LINDA ASH

Bellerin' and bawlin', yellin' and hollerin',
Rant and rave, cuss and swear,
Muck and mire burnin' hair,
Flyin' ropes, bawlin' calves,
Brandin' fires lots of laughs,
Bloody knives from notchin' ears,
Puttin' out fires on burnin' rears.
Brandin' comes just twice a year,
Wonder what I'm doin here?
Jammin' needles into hides,
Vaccinate to keep them alive.
Pokin' down pills to cure the ills,
Pourin' on stuff to kill the lice,
They say it's cheap at half the price.
Worked on now from head to rear,
Open the chute, get it out of here,
Weavin' and staggerin', bloody and burned,
Watchin' it go. One thing I've learned,
No matter how hard or how much I try,
That damn fool calf will probably die!

Bill Lowman is a visual artist, a poet, and a rancher from Sentinel Butte, North Dakota.

THE GREAT WANAGAN CREEK FLOOD

BILL LOWMAN

It was June fifteenth in nineteen eighty-four
Alfalfa on the bottoms was comin' in kinda poor

It clouded up fast then turned plumb black
We dropped off them cows and we hustled on back

Seven or eight inches can't say what it'd been
But it all came down in an hour shorta ten

It's known today as the Great Wanagan Creek Flood
A rollin' and rippin' and boilin' with mud

That hail was a steamin' in the hot summer air
Like fresh mornin' fog I'm witness to bear

My dad had a wild sorta look in his eyes
Never seen Wanagan a third this size

Amazed by its strength and flash of surprise
My ma stood there watchin' in darkness disguise

Early next mornin' we could finally forge
Nine fences were gone that crossed through its gorge

There was wire in the tree tops down by the mouth
I'm guessin' some posts went clear on south

With a stroke of good luck found no cows floatin' dead
Could have well been bankers' ink flowin' red

Cattle scattered like sixty years of no change
For a while it'll be all open range

Ross Knox has cowboyed in nine states. He has not only learned a large number of the old classic poems but also written much verse of his own.

SO LONG

ROSS KNOX

Well I was travelin' through the country
with a damned good friend of mine,
Just me and Buffalo and a dog named Hobo,
better pards you'll never find.

We woke up in Paradise* one mornin'
'twas a cold and drizzlin' day.
Betwixt the two of us we both decided
that we'd best be on our way.

We rolled our beds and packed our kacks*
with nothing in mind but getting gone.
We had one last drink for a fair ye well
then we bid those folks "so long."

We climbed on our outfit and fired it up,
a-fixin' on getting out.
We got that old red Chevy pickup
on a highway headed south.

'Twas about three o'clock one chilly morn,
but things was lookin' fine.
It was about that time that we crossed Hoover Dam
and struck that Arizona line.

We rolled it on into Kingman,
'bout as fast as that old pickup could fly.
We stayed at a dirty little run down motel,
a place called the Hualapai.

And we stayed with a friend in Wickenburg
for a couple of days, then moved on.
I had an old partner I wanted to see,
he was camped southeast of Tucson.

Well Rusty and Peggy McCorkell
were as fine a folks as you ever would meet.
When it comes to ropin' and tyin' cows,
Old Rusty is damned hard to beat.

Well I'd like to think they was glad to see us,
but most likely glad to see us gone.
We stayed a few days, then we pulled out,
and again it was just "so long."

We had us a bottle and we waved it around
till folks all thought we were insane.
By the time we hit the Interstate,
why Buffalo was feeling no pain.

Well he raised up the bottle and he made us a toast,
"In this cruel world we'll saunter forth."
When he sobered up he was feelin' homesick
so we headed the old pickup north.

Well up through Trinidad and on into Timpas,
just a little jerkwater town,
Then we pulled it on in at Buffalo's folks
about two hours after sundown.

Well we stayed for two weeks till just after Christmas
and a better Christmas I never had.
But we hired on ridin' some hot-blooded colts
so it was "so long" to his mom and dad.

Well they shipped us to Texas along with the colts,
and we stayed in an old winter shack.
But they run it like farmers and things didn't work out,
so we headed the old pickup back.

We went broke in Las Cruces in New Mexico state
and we starved for as long as we could,
But there weren't any jobs to be found anywhere
so we went to work cuttin' wood.

Well we cut wood for two weeks, eleven hours every day,
really a-feelin' harassed,
Till Buffalo got word that his dad needed help
so headed up toward the Wine Glass.*

Now we're working again but just for awhile,
and again before long we'll be gone.
Probably headed back south for some more warmer weather
and again it'll be "so long."

Paradise Paradise Vally, Nevada
kacks slang for saddle
Wine Glass the brand for a ranch in Elko County, Nevada

EASY CHAIRS
AND SADDLE SORES

ROSS KNOX

City folks sit back in their reclining chairs
And they thumb through a paperback book
By Louis Lamour or maybe Zane Grey,
And they contemplate how a cowboy should look.

He comes riding into town on a big black stud
With a gun hangin' off each hip,
And he'll shoot any man about three dozen times
Who commences to give him some lip.

Well he's broad across the shoulders with a 30-inch waist
And his arms is both made of steel.
To watch him clean house on twenty-five men in a barroom,
It just seems unreal.

He stays a few days, keepin' his gun hand in use,
Till he finally cleans out the crooks,
Then he settles down and marries the town sweetheart,
Well that's when you finish the book.

The bad guy's always ugly, with a week's growth of beard,
And the good guy's romantic as hell.
But I guess they can't write 'em no other way,
'Cause if they did these books wouldn't sell.

But there ain't nothing romantic in a cowpuncher's life,
No matter what people say;
He'll work hard all month with nothing ahead
But a night on the town come payday.

Now these fairy tale horses, they'll all watch a cow,
And slide at the touch of a rein,
They'll jump out and run and spin on a dime
And give you back seven cents change.

But you folks never heard a stampeding horse,
One that will buck at the drop of a hat,
He'll stumble and fall and leave you all busted up
And afoot on some barren flat.

I've seen men so crippled that they can't hardly walk
As they hobble out to the catch pen,
They'll rope out their pony and saddle him up
Just to see if they can't do it again.

Yet you can still sit and listen to some self-righteous folks
Cuss cowboys and the job that they do;
They say that the world it ought to be rid
Of such a sorry illiterate crew.

Yet I've worked around cowboys who dropped out of school,
Others with a college degree;
You never can tell when they step on a horse
Which one the best hand will be.

For that small piece of paper that you've got stashed away
That tells what you're qualified for
Ain't worth the paper that it's written on
When this feller steps across an old horse.

And you can't learn the tricks of a horse or a cow
By a sittin' and readin' some page.
It comes from hard work and more broken bones,
And a body that'll stiffen with age.

So just take a deep seat in that reclinin' chair,
Turn the pages on your paperback book.
Mix one more highball and set into thinkin'
On just how a cowboy should look.

THE DYING TIMES

ROSS KNOX

Any man makin' a living by punchin' cows
Will know what I mean when I say
The good times that's been had are comin' to an end;
Friends, we've about reached that day.

Old timers would say we just strike a long trot,
You couldn't load those old ponies in a truck,
But that was the day you'd step across an old horse
Without giving a damn whether he'd buck.

Now I guess for the rodeo man on the go,
A truck and a trailer's just fine,
But if you've noticed the tracks of a horse that's been hauled,
Well, he can't hardly walk a straight line.

I worked for an outfit up north one time
That never heard of a trot,
They'd load their old ponies to go two hundred yards
And spend an hour to find an unloadin' dock.

They'll tear up the saddle that you worked hard to get,
And it'll sure enough cripple the horse.
When you load and unload a dozen times every day,
The chances they start gettin' worse.

And for those who don't know what a good saddle costs,
They're about eight hundred dollars made plain,
And to have one tore up in five minutes time
To me seems a little insane.

Yet that ain't the point that I'm tryin' to make,
Though it sure enough come on as fast,
What I'm tryin' to say is in twenty more years
A cowboy could be a thing of the past.

And what about the youngsters that want to punch cows,
Now and then you'll find one or two,
When their time comes around, the chance may be gone,
'Cause good outfits are gettin' mighty few.

But for me and my partner and a few folks I know
It'd sure enough be just fine
If they'd invent a machine like I seen on T.V.
That would turn back the pages of time.

"Old Horse" is one of the hundreds of poems which regrets the loss of a loved horse. Don Ian Smith is a Methodist preacher and rancher.

OLD HORSE

DON IAN SMITH

Old faithful horse, I find you by the creek.
You try to stand, but you are much too weak.
I know the end has come for you at last;
Too many times has winter come, and passed;
Too many times we've heard the blackbird's call
In spring; watched summer turn to fall.
And I have tried before with pills and grain
To get you on those ancient feet again,
But I can tell this time it cannot be.
It's in the way you moan and look at me.

You've been a great old horse, all I could ask.
You've never backed away from any task
I've put you to. Sometimes it's quite a race
To keep each frisky yearling in her place
While trailing out the stock to summer grass;
And now it's finished; how the swift years pass.
You saw me bring my bride to the old shack
We once called home. On your strong trusty back
She learned to ride. My little ones in turn
Each knew your patient strength that helped them learn
To ride, and sit upon you straight and tall;
You've stopped and waited when they've had a fall.

So many years have come to take their toll
Since first you came, a bright-eyed little foal
By this same creek, to see the light of day;
To learn to run and buck and frisk and play.
When you were young and strong, you knew no fears,

But now it's been so many many years.
O God, I wonder why it has to be
This hard and lonely act is left for me?
Love leaves no choice as far as I can see
But quick and kindly death to set him free.

I'll get my gun down from the rifle rack.
Old friend, how many times you've had to pack
Some big old buck down off the steepest hill
When this same rifle made its smashing kill.
I'll blink away the salty, futile tears and
Forget a moment, all the pleasant years;
I could not stand the sense of foolish shame
I'd feel if blurring vision spoiled my aim.

It's hard for me to do this final task
And yet somehow I know it's all you ask.
I cannot leave you lying here to die
By inches, while impatient magpies fly
Around your drooping head. They will not wait
The dignity of death to seal your fate.
There's only one thing left for me to do,
And that's to send this bullet straight and true;
To smash your aching, aged, weary brain
And cut the snubbing rope of age and pain
That keeps your poor old body firmly bound
To this one little spot of frozen ground.

Melvin Whipple was born in Utah on a border ranch which straddled Arizona. He has lived and cowboyed in several western states and now works at a feedlot in Hereford, Texas.

OPEN RANGE

MELVIN L. WHIPPLE

I was born in Utah, many long years have come and gone
since Dad loaded up the wagon and we left that border town.
I don't quite remember, but I've heard my mother say,
we left sometime in April, or maybe it was May.

Mother said she drove the wagon while Dad drove the
                saddle stock,
we camped in old Quail Canyon 'mong the cedars, snow
                and rocks.
We left St. George, Utah, with our little caravan
headed south for Arizona, the golden, promised land.

I've heard it said in Arizona, in those days so long ago
they didn't lack for moisture, summer rains and winter snow.
The grass would drag your stirrups and 'twas sure a pretty sight
to watch the sun a sinkin' toward those hidden hills at night.

My Dad, he built a cabin and 'twas there we settled down,
they had come to make a fortune on a section of
                government ground.
Time has brought a lot of changes in that golden
                land of dreams
since they settled in the 20s with their saddle horse and team.

Then, the cattle roamed in thousands, many different
                markin' brands,
hundreds of wild horses grazed that enchanted land.
Sometimes in the evening you could hear so sharp and shrill
the whistle of a wild stallion as he watched you from a hill.

Then if you would watch him as he stood with head held high
you could see his nostrils flarin', pride burned those
		wicked eyes.
Then, again you heard him whistle and the echo
		from the sound
would roll out over the prairie, from the mountains
		would rebound.

Then, he would whirl and leave there, with his mane
		and tail a-flow,
with his ears pinned back for freedom, 'twas a thrill to
		watch him go.
Those days are gone forever. In my memory of the past
seems I hear the dying hoofbeats of the days that couldn't last.

As I'm sitting here and thinking, I fancy I can see
phantom pictures of the prairie, just the way it used to be.
I see the old chuck wagon, there's cowboys gathered 'round,
their coffee cups beside them as they wolf their supper down.

The morning stars are rising, I still hear the old cook roar,
"Roll out and get them horses, Boy, that's what you're
		hired for."
I'd crawl out of my blankets, always half asleep,
put on my hat and britches, as in the east the daylight creeps.

Before I got my boots on, I'd have to stomp around,
then I'd go untie the night horse, and pull my old hat down.
The horse would crouch and quiver and I was always
		some ashamed
the way my knees would tremble as I took the slack from
		the bridle reins.

I'd step up in the saddle and his head would drop from sight,
he'd buck and squeal and beller, put up one awful fight.
I tried to stay above him and spur him in the side,
and I want to tell you, Mister he learned this button
		how to ride.

As soon as he'd had his fun, Lord, how we'd go from there
a-flyin' through the sagebrush, how we split the morning air.
We had to have the horses before the day's work could begin
and there's no time I remember when we failed to bring
        them in.

Those good old days have vanished, far in the distant past,
but I've got a lot of memories of the times that couldn't last.
I still see those old cowboys, still hear the carefree yell
burned deep within my memories, the days I loved so well.

I fancy I'm sittin' on a cow horse, headin' down some
        rocky slope,
duckin', dodgin' cedars, a loop in my old grass rope.
The rocks would sure be rolling as we come off a
        mountain side,
a big steer out in the lead, just driftin' with the tide.

Those days are gone forever, only one place they're still at
is in some old man's memories underneath a greasy hat.
Mother and my sisters have long since moved to town,
my sisters they have scattered in different states around.

For many years Dad's been a-sleepin', out in his golden land,
no, there weren't no statues of him, all he had was
          work-worn hands.
But I know he is a-restin' for he went before the change,
now all I've left is memories of what once was open range.

VOICES IN THE NIGHT

MELVIN L. WHIPPLE

I've heard strange tales of haunted trails
Some folks believed 'twere true.
The things they told of spirits bold
The old-timers claimed they knew.

I didn't hold with the tales they told
Or their superstitious ways,
But I got my scare and I'll tell you fair,
I remember it to this day.

I feel it yet, the clammy sweat
And the cold chill up my spine.
'Twas in the spring and the grass was green
And the lonesome coyotes whined.

We slept on the floor with an open door,
My bed was against the wall.
A peaceful sleep and our lullaby
Was the owl and the nightbird's call.

The other three was breathin' free
When I woke with clammy chill.
I raised up in my bed and the cold sweat spread
And the night turned deathly still.

I strained my ears with the deathly fear
Which closed in on my chest.
I'm tellin' you, and I'll swear it's true,
I was almost scared to death.

Then I heard my name both clear and plain
Not thirty yards away.
The moon was full and the night was still
And the cabin light as day.

The others slept a peaceful sleep
But I sat with a frozen stare,
Then I heard a voice and it sounded close
Out in the night somewhere.

Terrified, I couldn't move,
Then another voice joined in.
I soaked in sweat while the others slept
And I strained to hear again.

Then I heard a tone, 'twas sort of a groan,
But I couldn't make out the words.
Then a cricket chirped and a pack rat raced
And I heard the call of a bird.

The night regained its usual sound
And I heard the others snore.
That heavy weight lifted from my chest
And I didn't sweat no more.

I've traveled many a lonesome trail
And I've often camped alone where
The whistling wind through the trees and rocks
Sounded like a ghostly moan.

I've rode rough trails on the blackest nights
When my horse refused to go,
He'd fight the bite and try to turn,
Paw and snort and blow;

But you couldn't put him past a tree
Or a certain place in the trail.
He'd work his ears with a deadly fear,
Snort and wring his tail.

I've seen a yearling's blood run free
Where a cougar made its kill,
And I've heard the mountain lion scream
A cry sharp and shrill.

I've heard the saddle carbine bark.
I've felt the breath of lead,
And I've awoken from a troubled dream
Sittin' straight up in my bed.

I've heard strange tales of haunted trails
But never believed 'twas true,
But someone called my name that night and
I was scared, I'm telling you.

I'd like to know who spoke to me
And why did they call my name.
Was it a phantom soul on a night patrol,
And why did it sound so plain?

Writing poetry has been a tradition in the Whipple family for five generations. This one was written by Melvin's son Lucky.

CHOOKALOSKI MARE

LUCKY WHIPPLE

Got entered in the broncs
At the Coconino fair,*
Reservations for a flight out
On the Chookaloski* mare.

She ain't no virgin in the chute,
Plumb always on the fight.
And I knows when we gets airborne
This ain't gonna be no champagne flight.

Well I sets my saddle way up high
And measured off my reins.
Got down and called, "Let's have a horse,
Gonna roach this old hide's mane."

Then we went across the threshold and
I commenced to holdin' hair.
Just me and my high rollin' kack
And that Chookaloski mare.

She's lungin' and she's plungin',
I can shorely feel she's there,
She's Satan's favorite mistress,
That Chookaloski mare.

My bronc was sure a-hummin'
And I'm floatin' on the swell,
And I'm raisin' her from eyeballs
To the roots of her broom tail.

Well the ride was finally over,
The buzzer sounded loud,
From them Siouxpie Indians whoopin'
I know'd it pleased the crowd.

Never have I covered
Such an ignorant trashy wreck.
I had epileptic symptoms,
And I damn near broke my neck.

Then I missed a stroke and left her,
I knowed that was bound to hurt.
Then I rendered me a crater
In that Arizona dirt.

'Twas a damn fine classy ride,
Knowed I'd win without a doubt.
Then the announcer called out, "Goose egg,
Good ride, but he missed her out."

Finally picked my tattered frame up
From that old arena sod,
And I looked right up to heaven
And I said these words to God:

"If you've got any rough stock
In that holy land up there,
I'd be mighty much beholden,
Lord, ship that Chookaloski mare."

Well, I rattled out of Flagstaff,
Never will go back there,
Cause they don't give no reservations
On that Chookaloski mare.

Coconino Fair a county fair with an annual rodeo in Flagstaff, Arizona
Chookaloski a true life Indian-named female horse in the bucking contest of
the rodeo

BUCKIN' HORSE BALLET

LUCKY WHIPPLE

The Jigger Boss* hollered horses
As the Jingler* fogged 'em in,
Then reached down fer his hemp line*
With an evil sort'a grin.

With the speed of a strikin' rattler
The hoolihan* was thrown,
And the loop flowed out and guillotined
Round the throat lach of a roan.

Then he reeled him from the cavvy,*
One coil at a time,
And said, "New Man, bring yer hobbles,
We wanna hear yer tangos* chime."

With his head up like a cobra
And his tail rolled in a nine,
The roan stepped out stiff-legged,
Nostrils rollin' down the line.

Said I, "Yer plenty forked,* Son,
This bronc's named Angel Dust
And he'll fly you t'ward the heavens,
But he's all yours, in God we trust."

The new hand's tongue was silent,
But his actions spoke his skill.
He screamed as he caught his stirrup
Like a she lion on the kill.

Ol' Angel Dust erupted
Like a marlin from the deep,
But the twister set atop of him,
Calm as a chimney sweep.

The blue roan wadded tightly,
Like a viper at recoil,
Then lashed out like a switch blade
And plunged his four feet in the soil.

We all watched in awe and witnessed,
The exhibition had certainly begun,
As ol' Angel and that twister
Rose above the risen sun.

Then the roan hit spraddle-legged
And his head emerged for air
As the north Nevada breeze
Swept off the dust and floatin' hair.

There was bear sign on ol' Angel
And the blood oozed from his hide.
He looked like a spring-toothed harrow
Had been dragged down either side.

The Angel looked defeated,
His skirmish came to cease,
Then a meadowlark broke the stillness
With his harmonizing peace.

Ain't no fancy New York dancers,
With their theatrical display,
That can match the grace and beauty
Of a buckin' horse ballet.

Jigger Boss a Nevada term for cowboy boss
Jingler an old term for horse wrangler when strings of horses wore bells
hemp line lariat or rope of hemp fibers
hoolihan backhand thrown loop for roping horses
cavvy from the Spanish *caviet*, which means a string of horses
tango spurs
forked bow-legged bronc rider

Gordon Eastman composed this poem after he was cited for riding his horse through his hometown city park in Lewistown, Montana, formerly called Buckskin Flats.

BUCKSKIN FLATS

GORDON EASTMAN

No hoofprints planned
To mark this land
Where buffalo once made their last stand

Where deer and elk and antelope grazed
Where their young were born and the young were raised
As watchful mothers in the warm sun lazed

It knew that the calvary horse and the bullet's whine
The Indian pony and the arrow's rock tine
And saw a reluctant retreat to a distant line

The homeless Metis* then camped this ground
And their hobbled ponies did wide a-bound
To seek the forage which their hunger found

Here herds of cattle and sheep put on weight
To fight and play and propagate
With the water they drank and the grass they ate

Then the nester* came with his fences and plows
And sore-shouldered horses filled bins and mows
From the lands intended for grazing cows

Here the old time circus pitched their tents
Huge Clydes and Percherons left their dents
As Tom Mix's Tony and the elephants

To the realtor's eye it was subdivide
Into nice square lots and a park real wide
Thus no trails left for a kid to ride

Blacktopped roads now run its girth
And motored wheels now weight the earth
But no hoof touches this guarded turf

Courts and fields in their alloted space
The litter of humans' careless waste
War relics and fences now mark the place

Where tribal councils met in session
To make the rules and make decisions
And no rule made without good reason

Metis a northern tribe of Indians whose lineage is native and French Canadian
Nester term for homestead farmers who settled on the western lands

Duane Reece comes from a ranching family that takes great pride in working with the wildest cows on the roughest land.

No Imposter

DUANE REECE

She was coming three, her hide was slick,
    untouched by human hand.
In her short life she learned all the tricks
    to beat her rugged land.

Her mamma died, as tough a cow
    as a range had ever had.
A brahma bull, that ran far below,
    was both grandpappy and her dad.

Her feet were sharp, her flanks were high,
    her horns grew long and keen.
She had all the lines, both blood and build,
    to be a wildcow queen.

It was her time of year, the feed was strong,
    flies were not a pest,
and she'd have been content, if left alone,
    just to eat and rest.

But for days on end, she'd ran and hid,
    like taught since birth to do,
when those smelly boogers, with wicked ways,
    would come by in a day or two.

This time they'd stayed, had made life hard,
    and her bunch begin´to thin.
They'd disappear, those dogs were quiet,
    then here they'd come again.

She'd escaped with ease, but something said,
    "Move now or it's the end."
She circled and bawled, for two long nights,
    with no answer from her kin.

It said, "Turn up, till it climbs no more,
    higher than you've ever been.
Graze only at night, thirst you fight,
    and be ready to run again."

She'd rim for a while, wandered about,
    she'd stop and look back down.
She'd sniff the breeze, herd instincts strong,
    but always upward bound.

In a last lone bush, she was in her den,
    with ledge hung overhead
where she found, that once before,
    a cow had made a bed.

In a still damp spot, where last week's snow
    filled a limestone crack,
with two week's beard on last sound horse,
    a cowboy found her track.

He'd prowled since the dawning, all alone,
    was free to roam
since two days before, with sign played out,
    he'd sent his pardner home.

He was stiff and sore, he eased to ground,
    loosened up his kack
He shook it some, propped it up,
    and aired his pony's back.

He belched up his last night's coffee, that
    warmed for breakfast tasted bad.
He wished to hell he'd eat somethin else,
    if somethin else he had.

His wood all gone, he still had coals,
    the moon gave a little light.
The works were done, he'd dumped the pot,
    he was headed in tonight.

To hobbled horse he'd fed end of grain,
    tied last sorefooted dog.
He thought, I'll make just one more round
    to jump that white musshog.

The time he'd spent, tracks he'd made,
    he'd rather been held and hooked.
And a-way up high, in them dirty roughs,
    the one place he hadn't looked.

Now he cinched his beat-up saddle,
    pulled down hat and hitched his chaps
He groaned astride, rimmed on around
    the mountain's solid caps.

Sometimes he wished his days would end
    on another lay of land
where the cattle there, when you rode by,
    just look up and stand.

Or where water's scarce, and triggers work,
    or just round up with hay,
And the main concerns, the buyer's cut,
    and what'er they gonna weigh.

The race was on, she'd got the jump,
    her kind travel light.
He'd seen her back, a toppin out,
    then drop out of sight.

He'd paid his dues a thousand times,
    this wasn't runnin ground.
Most cows roped here would likely be,
    in windies heard in town.

And to lead off here, it could be done,
    but he'd have it awful slow,
So the thing to do was save his gas,
    and make his coup below.

He'd stay in sight, not too close,
    let her pick the way
On the cholla mesa, between mountain and moat,
    he'd overtake her play.

Sixty minutes of hurry, three thousand feet down,
    five miles of rough and limb,
She'd stopped twice, turned broadside,
    and had a look at him.

They were almost there, he found a blind,
    the going pretty good.
He half-hit a lope, would steal some gap,
    or at least he hoped he could.

So far so good, her trot was the same,
　　a free and easy roll.
He reached down, found his latigo,*
　　and pulled up another hole.

Now she'd looked back, he hung the steel,
　　threw away all dread,
Green was splashed up at the top,
　　now rocks were specked with red.

His lifetime catch, led head to tail,
　　would reach across the state,
But one like her, he seen right quick,
　　he hadn't tried of late.

A speed machine, like few he'd run
　　in many a cowboy year,
With a fluid drive she could coast a jump,
　　and hit a higher gear.

On the gentle slope, breaths were short,
　　he slowly gained on her.
On a radar gun, his travel rate would have read
　　near forty per.

Then he'd see a chance, take a swing,
　　a bad'un she'd find.
He'd try to dodge, lose his go,
　　and be six lengths behind.

He had to cheat, cut across,
　　let her come to him.
The place to meet, coming fast,
　　the break in outer rim.

He took a lay, sitting flat,
　　fouled by thorny weight,
His loop hung dead, on the tip of a horn,
　　in a hatsize figure-eight.

Her wind was broke, she rolled and fell,
    along with dust and din,
but where she'd light, in the river's hair,
    the bulge was hers again.

Off the edge of the earth he had to go,
    not give her time to hide.
With tail of rope he helped his cause,
    Leaned back into the ride.

At the end of his reins he hunkered down,
    her crackling line of flight.
In his face the thicket stood,
    reared up for the fight.

He damned his luck, for one green pup
    he'd give half his herd,
But all he had was what he was,
    cowboy is the word.

No time to hunt, he made a hole,
    run blind through hidden bogs,
Beat his way with blackened ribs,
    jumped drifts, and fallen logs.

The reaching snags, his rigging broke,
    he ducked the hornet's whine.
His seat went down, his jumper ripped,
    half hung by drooping vine.

Then light ahead, a thrashing dive,
    the cold swimming glide,
He looked ahead, wet clods were there
    on the river's sunny side.

Wet and feathered with trash, mouth burned dry,
    horse with ringing tail.
The win was his, he'd caught a glimpse,
    again he wouldn't fail.

His hat and glasses, odds and offal,
    lay back along his wake.
But these tough'uns cleaned, for awhile, with one
    more jump to take.

With his bleeding nose, glassy eyes,
    dallies in trembling hand.
These ways of his, some folks he knew,
    just wouldn't understand.

But he planned to never weaken, from what told,
    that long-lost day.
"Son always ride, with the mortal fear,
    that one might get away."

latigo a buckled strap to which the cinch is attached, or a type of leather tanning

Harold Otto has watched his country near Pateros, Washington, turn from cattle country to apple orchards.

COWS AND LOGS

HAROLD OTTO

For many years I herded cows
Upon the dusty trails.
I've throwed my rope around their horns
And twisted on their tails.
I have cussed them in the Spring and Fall,
In Winter's freezing days,
And wound up broke by Christmas time
In a line shack feeding hay

To a bunch of cows that seemed to know
Just how to make me mad.
And anything that bothered me
Seemed to make them glad.
Then I heard about a logger's life
In the woods of Puget Sound,
Of the money paid for little work,
And of the girls in town.

So I threw my saddle on my horse
And bid the cows goodbye.
I sang a song as I rode away
For the land with timber high.
One summer day I reached my goal
Not far from Snohomish town,
Getchell is what it was called
And the boss I soon had found.

He said that he would put me on
As help was rather short,
But as he looked my outfit o'er
I thought I heard him snort.
He eyed my spurs and high-heeled boots,
My Stetson and my jeans,
Then said "My boy, when morning comes
You'll see just what I mean."

When morning came and breakfast o'er
I soon appeared for work.
A logger's strife my aim in life,
No duty would I shirk.
The boss soon took me in tow,
He said I'd work on foot of course.
I wondered what a man could do
Without a saddle horse.

He took me to a pile of rope,
The stuff was made of steel.
Too stiff to braid a hondo* in
Or rope a critter's heel.
He said, "Just take a coil of that
To the donkey in the woods,
But you better take your spurs off first,
In the brush they're just no good."

With rope in hand I walked awhile,
But no donkey could I see.
Just a big iron thing blowing smoke
Fastened to a tree.
With steel ropes going everywhere
What an awful racket it made,
I couldn't of heard the donkey,
Even if he had brayed.

I walked around the woods till noon
And then I saw the boss.
He said, "My boy, where have you been,
Or were you only lost?"
He said, "The donkey needs that line,
You take it there right now."
I said, "Where is the donkey at?
I will rope him like a cow."

He looked amazed and pointed to
The iron thing blowing smoke.
Then said, "My boy, I only hope
You are not playing a joke."
I said, "No sir, it is no joke,
Of that you have no fear.
The only kind of donkey I know
Has four legs and long ears."

And then I saw him kinda grin,
He seemed alright somehow.
He said, "You sure don't know the woods,
But I never saw a cow."
We shook hands then and parted friends,
I threw my saddle on my horse
And started back to the bunch grass hills
To punch more cows, of course.

So, punchers, just take my advice,
Don't yearn for pastures green.
And don't believe the stranger's tales
Of places he has seen.
Just stay at home where you belong,
For riches do not hope.
You'll find in life there's things much worse
Than cow dung on your rope.

hondo or honda, the eye in one end of a rope into which the other end goes
to make a loop

Vern Morensen has ranched and herded sheep in the country all around his home in Parowan, Utah.

RANGE COW IN WINTER

VERN MORTENSEN

Have you listened still on a desert hill
  At the close of a bitter day,
When the orange sun in wispy clouds
  Was set in a greenish haze?
In a cold white world of deepening drifts
  That cover the land like a pall,
Then the plaintive bawl of a hungry cow
  Is the loneliest sound of all!

Have you listened still on a desert hill
  When the world was cold and drear,
When the tinkling bells of a herd of sheep
  Was the nearest sound you'd hear,
And the haunting notes of a lone coyote whose
  Evening's hunting howl

Rose wild and clear in the cold blue night,
    And was answered by the hoot of an owl?

But when the scanty grass lies covered deep
    By the snow that lies like a pall,
Then the plaintive bawl of a hungry cow
    Is the loneliest sound of all!

---

*In this poem, R. O. Munn of Baker, Oregon, relates a true experience of
his youth.*

YOUNG FELLERS

R . O . MUNN

A buddy and I left home
One fine summer's day.
Objective—a cow punching job,
Found one puttin' up hay.
We'd made it to Jordan Valley,
Our finances were getting low.
It was the 4th of July,
And they were havin' a rodeo.

Between us we had enough
For just one entrance fee,
And so it was decided
The participant would be me.
I picked bull ridin' since
I'd rode a few milk cows,
Which was stretching it a little,
About as much as the law allows.

We camped out that night
Near the rodeo ground
With nothin' to eat, but
Thinking our fortune was found.
We got up next morning,
The day was bright and clear,
And for breakfast we divided
A can of lukewarm beer.

Shortly things got started
And real festivities begun.
I went to look for my bull,
He was in chute number one.
Big, brawny and brindle,
A mean look on his white face
And a huge hump on his shoulders
That sorta looked out of place.

Finally my turn came and
I crawled down inside.
My short legs stuck straight out,
His back was so wide.
I pulled my hat down,
Took a big chew of snoose.
Last wrap, nodded my head, and
They turned the old boy loose.

He left the terra firma
In one tremendous bound,
And swingin' his head from side-to-side
Started gyratin' around.
At the height of his leap he
Changed tactics and suddenly spun
And I sailed through the air
Like I had been shot from a gun.

I landed flat on my belly,
My shirttail hangin' loose.
My eyes were full of dirt,
And I had swallowed all my snoose.
As I staggered to my feet,
Someone hollered, "Look out!"
That old bull was headed my way.
He meant business, no doubt.

Now I'll never know
How I made that top rail
While the bull pawed dirt
And fanned the air with his tail.
He took after the clowns,
Scattered the crowd,
And as he left the arena
He was still lookin' proud.

I rubbed a few sore spots,
Thinking there must be better ways.
I'd had enough bull ridin'
To last all my days.
Well I guess I survived,
But please believe this narrator:
The next rodeo I attend,
I'll be a paying spectator.

Drummond Hadley is a well-known university-trained poet who ranches on the Arizona-Mexico border.

GATHERING CATTLE IN THE DEERTRACKS PASTURE

DRUMMOND HADLEY

No wind, still the dry side-oat's stems are swaying.
In the winter sunlight on the pale dust, listen . . .
Hear the still rangeland ringing in your ears.

My dun horse swings his head toward the first click of hooves.
Vaqueros* trailing a herd through the sands of the arroyo* bed
Drift by calling "picale, ándale, ir'ya vacas."*

Blue sky and the bald Peloncillo Mountains ahead,
a rocky trail behind. Come on dun horse,
there's still a long way left to ride

                    till daylight's gone and the work is done.

Vaqueros Mexican word for cowboy
arroyo canyon
picale, andale, ir'ya vacas "cows, get a move on"

Dick Gibford grew up in California where his father taught horsemanship, and since then has been buckarooing in Nevada, Idaho and Oregon.

THE OLD COWMAN

DICK GIBFORD

There's many types and sizes,
With their odd and unique forms,
Among the human beings that do differ
From our average status norms.

There is a weathered fellow,
Somewhat cautious and reserved,
Who struggles for survival
With his humor and his nerve.

I've had occasion to observe him
In the city where the hypnotic rush is swift,
Just a-trailing along in the traffic,
Plumb content just to drift.

Or on the sidewalk wet and gritty
A-walkin' in the rain,
His face pure bliss enlightment
Contrasted to others in their pain.

Or in a cafe in the swelter
Of a hot midsummer's day,
Drinking coffee hot and steaming,
His forehead white and gleaming,

Sombrero pushed way back
Shaded up until the sun set
Before he makes another track.

No matter where I've noticed
This fellow brother hangin' loose among the grind,
A certain quality of composure
Persists within his soul and mind.

And his homespun education
May some day serve humanity,
As to how to live together
In peace to some degree.

But for now he goes his own way,
A master of himself,
Teaching from example,
His knowledge on the shelf.

And his face is aged and wrinkled,
His eyes are narrow slits,
His legs are stiff and side sprung
Where his horse and saddle fits.

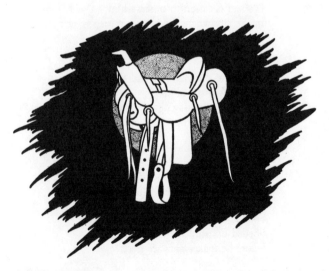

And the elemental forces
Have shaped his outer bark to suit,
But like the gnarled old desert juniper,
You can't discount the root.

Extracting and exacting
The miracle of life,
Until the measure of its treasures
Is honed, like a surgeon's knife

And can operate on others
With precision and delight.
And down on through the ages,
The sifting time-worn sands
Have fallen silent witness
To this old cowman.

COWBOY'S TOAST

DICK GIBFORD

Here's to the best of the good
And the worst of the bad,
All them old horses I rode
Since I was a lad.

To the do's and the don'ts
And the why's and the not's,
And all them round-up cooks
A-scrubbin' out their iron pots,

And the blizzard that bites,
And the sun that grows grass,
And the saddle that wears a hole
In your pants,

To the high lonesome deserts
And timbered peaks,
And the smell of your hide
When you ain't bathed for weeks,

To the warm summer breeze
At first light of day,
And the wild nights in town
When you gather your month's pay,

To the ladies that dance
To the tune of the juke,
And the sight of the pickup
All stained with dust,

And the rough, rocky road back to camp,
Tobacco that's spilt,
And the papers that's damp,
And the long hot dry circle
You ride the next day,
A-thinkin' real hard on changin' your ways.

And here's to your health
When you're back on your feet,
All the ridin' and ropin'
Done up so neat.

Way out in the brush
Where no one can see,
To the burnin' hair
At the brandin' bee.

And those oysters that's et
Direct from the fire,
All flavored with ashes
And sagebrush smoke.
And here's to your life-long desire
Whether you're rich
Or whether you're broke,

To the peace in your mind
When you reach your goal,
To the truth in your heart
And the wealth in your soul.

And let's toast to the trail blazers,
Wherever they be,
Their genius and courage
That made us so free.

And the greatest artists
Down through the years,
The Russells and the Phippins,
And last frontiers.

And here's joy to the present
And to the future with hope,
And the quick dally velta*
At the end of the rope.

dally velta see "Sierry Petes"

THE LAST BUCKAROO

DICK GIBFORD

By morning star and quarter moon
And day's growing light,
A cowboy and his trusty steed
Are ambling into sight.

The night is gone, a day is born,
The world keeps spinnin' on,
A cowboy and his trusty steed
Are movin' in the dawn.

Cattle on a thousand hills,
There's a cowboy on a few,
Gathering to the rodeer grounds
Comes the last buckaroo.

The sun is a-high up in the sky,
The herd is settling down,
There's a cowboy and his trusty steed,
They're movin' round and round.

The irons are hot,
A slick un's caught and taken to the fire,
A cowboy and his trusty steed
Are earning well their hire.

The branding's done,
The day was fun,
The time it fairly flew.
Ridin' back to the cow camp
Comes the last buckaroo.

How can the times be so amiss,
Can all we know be what we read?
Beyond the tickin' of the clock and chimes
Comes a cowboy and his steed.

This human race
That we embrace
We're usin' up all space,
Super powers,
They lie for hours,
Right to each other's face.

The truth seems lost,
How can the cost
Be worth what we paid?
By living fast,
Before the mast
Of a ship sunk every day.

The urbanite
Has taken flight
Not knowin' where to roost,
The dollar bill
Has changed his will,
And given him a boost.

The first be last,
The last be first,
Comes the echo of the day,
While modern man who is of this world
Is crowding for his pay.

Yet far from the traffic jam
I see,
Beyond the desert's rim,
A cowboy and his trusty steed
A-moving after him.

The bell she tolls
For all our souls,
Be thee what they may.
She always has been truer than
The wise men of the day.

The king and queen of hearts,
They know what to do,
Ridin' lead to Armageddon
Comes the last buckaroo.

The first to fight
For what is right,

Don Quixote is immortal,
The ship is lost
When at sea she's tossed
And she's sinkin' to the portals.

Yet I see
Past bravery
And heroism at its best,
Genghis Khan's
Long since gone,
Laid himself to rest.

The time is now
For truth indeed.
A-driftin' with the cattle
Comes the cowboy and his steed,
A-fightin' their own battle.

Hooves of old,
Sure, hooves so bold,
Iron shod hooves within the lead
Close behind the dust,
Hell bent or bust
Comes a cowboy and his steed.

The patriots,
The well-worn ruts
Of flaming candid ardour,
There's a gentry in the country
With plain disdain for foolish martyrs.

Yet I don't pretend
To lend
Much solace to the race,
But with a heart that's true,
The last buckaroo,
Is standing in his place.

Bill Simpson lives and works in the bends of the Snake River Valley where he has written some of the most telling observations about cowboy life in his part of the country

THE GLOW

BILL SIMPSON

Well, what's in a fire
That pulls a man's desire
To stare a hard gaze
At a campfire blaze?

From the bright amber coals
To where the blue flame rolls,
The glow is sure there,
And it'll draw your stare.

Men set for hours
While the red flame flowers
Without a thought in their head,
Like their mind's gone dead.

No want and no care,
It'll just hold you there
In a blank state of mind
With nothing to find.

Well the poppin' and crackin'
Goes on unobserved,
It's the flames
That hold you so reserved.

They're leapin' and reachin'
And tryin' to find
A way to penetrate
Man's simple mind.

LIKE IT OR NOT

BILL SIMPSON

Me and the boys
was a-drinkin' our fill
At the old buckaroo bar,
Up there on the hill.

We was bein' pretty quiet
An' doin' real well,
When the door came open
An' things went to Hell.

An old drunk cowboy
Stepped through the door,
He staggered an' stumbled,
Then fell on the floor.

He picked hisself up
An' kinda looked all around,
He staggered to the bar
An' he set himself down.

He was little an' thin,
An' bent and old,
Hard twisted and gray,
An' his eyes, they was cold.

His Levis was dirty,
But his white shirt was clean.
He had a look about him
You could almost call mean.

Well the crease in his hat
It was crooked and worn
An' the toes of his boots
Was an old cow's horn.

He didn't want to talk,
That was plain to show,
But the ol buckeroo knew
What I wanted to know.

So I bought him a beer
To bide me time,
I was wanting stories
To write me a rhyme.

When he finally got talking
On the beer he was allowed,
Yeah, the old buckaroo,
He was still mighty proud.

He said, "I rumbled and rambled
An' crashed through life.
I never had the courage
To take me a wife."

He said, "Life is hard,
It's tough at its best,
Then they lay you down
For that ever long rest."

He talked about women,
Puppies and babies,
The ifs, an's and buts,
An' all the maybes.

He told it plain,
Simple and true,
The dirty tough life
Of an old buckaroo.

"Well, the days and nights
Are lonely, you know."
About ropin', brandin', an'
No place to go.

About drinkin' and fightin'
An' ridin' 'em hard,
About fate he called luck
In the turn of a card.

About dust, rain and snow
An' the long endless nights,
About Old Blue and Old Rony,
And the tough old bull fights.

About the she-devil wind
The Lord had it blow,
He even talked about things
That he didn't know.

About his old Ford pickup
So faithful and true,
About the junk in the back
An' the women he'd knew.

About friends long gone,
His buckaroo pals,
An' a couple more times
He mentioned the gals.

About the camp up Jarbidge,*
The one south of Bend,
What it would be like
When he come to the end.

About the changes he'd saw
Through his long life,
An' you could tell he regretted
Not takin' a wife.

About the good old days,
An' how long they'd been gone,
The way things were now,
How could they go on?

Well the story was easy,
I'd heard it, you bet,
But the last thing he told me
I couldn't forget.

He told it so softly
With a tear in his eye,
He said, "Son, life's a bitch,
An' then you just die."

Jarbidge a mountain range in Nevada

Barney Nelson lives with her husband on the 06 Ranch near Alpine, Texas, where she writes and takes photographs. Her work regularly appears in Western Horseman *magazine.*

COWBOY'S FAVORITE

BARNEY NELSON

When a man spends his life on horseback,
And the country's been his home,
There are things he learns to love
As across the range he roams.

There's the scent of burning cedar
And the rhythmic windmill creak,
The song of a friendly mockingbird,
And sunshine on his cheek.

There's the smell of boiling coffee
Or a lonely coyote call,
The smell of sweaty horseflesh
And a lost calf's mournful bawl.

The light from a kerosene lamp
And the early flow'rs in spring,
These are but a few of
A cowboy's favorite things.

But there's one thing that the cowboy
Loves more than all the rest,
That makes him glad to be alive
And puts strength in his breast.

It's not the song that a fiddle plays
Or the money in his jeans.
It's not a brand new pair o' boots
Or a pot of pinto beans.

It's the promise from the Foreman,
Who rules the Range on High,
That the cows will once more fatten
And that the short grass will not die.

This smell that every cowboy loves,
No matter what the season,
And this sound that chases frowns away
No matter what the reason,

Is a simple thing that fills his heart
With peace from crib to cane,
The gift that brings life to his home,
The sound and smell of rain.

Jim Bollers farms near Hudson, Colorado.

FILL UP THOSE GLASSES, BARTENDER

JIM BOLLERS

You've got lots of beer, wine and whiskey,
Have you got any women who sell?
I've been out on the range for a long time, Boys,
and I'm feelin' frisky as hell.

So fill up all of those glasses, Bartender.
Hey Cowboys, put your money away,
'cause I'm going to tell you right now, I'm a spender,
and I've been savin my wages to pay.

To pay for just this one evenin'
I've been lookin' forward to for so long,
And I'd sure hate like hell
to make this here evenin' go wrong.

All I want is a bottle to empty.
All I want is a woman who'll dance.
I want all you boys to know somethin' right now,
I want you to know here in advance,

The last damn thing I want is trouble now,
The last damn thing I want to do is fight.
So let's all proceed with this evening now,
and hope to hell everything works out right.

So fill up all those glasses, Bartender,
I said fill them up to the brim,
and then you turn the music way up loud
and you turn the lights down dim.

Well, Honey, have you ever longed for a man to be tender?
Your prayers have been answered tonight.
And you already know I'm a spender, Darling,
and I intend to treat you just right.

So fill up all of those glasses, Bartender.
Hey Darlin', let's dance for a while.
Now you've got the prettiest red dress that I ever did see,
And you're just beautiful when you smile.

I'm sure glad I came here tonight,
And I'm so happy you dance my style,
and you're built like a million dollars, Woman,
and you're beautiful when you smile.

Mister, you know I've been feelin' real bad here lately.
In fact I'd have to get better to die.
But for some reason I keep livin',
Although I'm not really sure why.

Well, Mister, I am going to hell in a hurry,
Now that should be plain for you to see.
And I'd damn sure hate to take you with me, Mister,
but by God I will if you mess with me.

So let me apologize to your missus, Mister,
And you just put away that big long shiny knife.
Why, hell, I thought she was your sister, Mister,
I never dreamed she was your wife.

So fill up all those glasses, Bartender.
Hey cowboys, put your money away
Cause I'm going to tell you right now, I'm a spender,
And I've just been looking forward to today.

So let all of the booze flow freely.
Let the music loudly play.
There will probably be no tomorrow,
And who the hell cares about yesterday.

Owen Barton runs a ranch which straddles the Idaho-Nevada border.
His poems take a philosophical look at life in the saddle.

EARLY MORNING ROUNDUP

OWEN BARTON

Have you ever saddled your horse
And been on your way
When the hoot owls were hootin'
At the break of day?

And rode out on the range
In the real early morn'
And felt kinda' lucky
That you had been born?

Heard a meadow lark singin'
A real special tune,
With the stars fading out,
Though you can still see the moon.

Sagebrush and grass
Still sparklin' with dew,
The sky in the east is
Turning red, mixed with blue.

Your horse's shod hooves
Knock sparks from the rocks,
And you hear the strange struttin' sounds
Of them proud old sage cocks.

The lonesome wail
Of a coyote cry,
With nose pointed up
Toward the sky.

An eagle soars high,
With wings out-spread.
The sun's now coming up,
And it's sure big and red.

A red-tailed hawk screamin'
Down from the hill,
Looking for breakfast,
A rabbit to kill.

A magpie sits in a bush close by
Watching this with a watchful eye,
He'd like to enjoy a feast
With his brothers from the sky.

A horny toad struggles
To get out of your way,
A lizard glides off a rock
Like he wants to play.

Your horse shies off the trail
At the buzz of a rattle,
Then you sorta' remember
You're here to round up cattle.

Soon you jump some cows and calves
That take off on a run,
'Tis then you get to thinking
Cowboyin's nuthin' but fun.

Your horse is still fresh
And rarin' to go,
You're glad they are wild
And as yet ain't too slow.

You see an old bull bellerin'
And pawin' up dirt,
Then you take down your rope
To use as a quirt.

This is the way a roundup
Starts out on the range,
But along about noon
It all seems to change.

You've rode a big circle
Got them cows in a bunch,
Your breakfast's long gone
And you ain't got no lunch.

The sun sure is blazin'
Up high in the sky,
Your lips are startin' to crack
They're gettin' so dry.

The water holes you've seen
Ain't fit to drink,
They're gettin' so stale
They're startin' to stink.

You still can remember
That beautiful morn,
But the grin on your face
Has turned to forlorn.

You got the cows corraled
And have started to brand.
There's plenty of work,
For every last hand.

The air's full of smoke
From the burnin' of hair,
And you're so damn tired
You don't even care.

Your throat starts to burn
From so much bitter smoke,
And your lungs fill with dust
Till you think you will choke.

Your hands are covered with blood
From earmarkin' ears,
And changin' bull calves
Into castrated steers.

Cows and calves bawlin'
In a loud steady roar,
It could only be louder
If there were more.

By the time the last calf
Is wearin' a brand,
You are dusty and sweaty
And your boots full of sand.

Then you open the gate
And let out a yell,
And they all stampede out
Like they were just leavin' hell.

Then you hold 'em in a bunch
Till the calves find their mothers.
With a brand on the hip
They all look like the others.

But them old cows know
By the smell of the hide,
And each soon has her own
Trottin' off by her side.

You've darn near forgot
About that beautiful morn,
And how lucky you were
That you had been born.

Can't even remember
The meadow lark's song,
And you wonder how such a beautiful day
Could go wrong.

Your muscles all ache
And your butt's kinda' sore,
But at daybreak tomorrow
You'll be ready for more.

You'll be wantin' to hear
That old coyote howl,
And watch the day break
At the hoot of an owl.

You'll again want to see
That old horny toad
As he plows through the dust
To get out of your road.

Again see the eagle
As he soars in the sky,
And you'll hope you're a cowboy
Till the day that you die.

My Ol' Stetson

OWEN BARTON

When you look upon this ol' Stetson hat
You can tell it has been where the action was at.
I look at it with a lot of pride
'Cause it went wherever I had to ride.

It's been all over the Diamond A
And added to comfort all the way.
It's been stomped and tromped into the dirt,
Been used as a hazer and also a quirt,

Has shielded my eyes from the desert sun
And has helped me along, when I had to run.
It's been used to water my thirsty hoss,
And been a sign to all that I am boss.

Protected my face from storm and sleet,
Even been used to warm cold feet.
Has helped me to turn a wild old cow,
Please don't ask me to tell you how.

When a mean ol' bull was blowin' snot,
This old hat has helped a lot.
There was just no way that it could hurt,
But it made him stop a-pawin' dirt.

It's helped sack out a lotta' broncs,
Even been worn in honky tonks.
Been used as a pillow, and a shade for my eyes
When the sun was hot in the blazin' skies.

Spattered with dehorning blood, dirt and grease,
It served its purpose and is now at peace.
Hanging here so all alone,
The best damn thing a man could own.

So when I go to the other side,
And am lucky enough to have a horse to ride,
I hope this old Stetson will meet me there.
If it don't, St. Peter sure ain't fair.

*Don Bell has rodeoed and run rough stock all his life. He lives in the
Big Horn Basin near Byron, Wyoming.*

GOING TO THE
SHAWNEE RODEO

DON BELL

I was fightin' this Model T through the Oklahoma clay,
The kids all squallin', God what a day.
Had it in low gear, revved up damn tight,
Them magneto lamps give a bright light.

She wouldn't take high, so I kept 'er in low,
We was headin' fer Shawnee, to a darn Rodeo.
I had seven kids and this Indian wife,
Then I was young, and thought this is the life.

I'd stopped at a bootleggers, bought some home brew,
The old woman didn't like it, but said it would do.
She was already drunk, and I was getting tight.
Still had 'er in low, going through the night.

The kids ate all the bologna and right damn quick
Three was pukin', and the rest pretty sick.
The old Ford was a missin', hittin' on three
So I stopped in the mud, and let all the kids pee.

I had side curtains on but the wind blew in,
The old lady was drunk, wearing this silly grin,
She said we better stop soon, and get a jug o' corn,
'Cause I'm getting drunk shor'n your born.

I'm mad as all hell, guess you can see,
We are blessed, Dear Don, cause I'm sure I'm P. G.
I told you damn plain, we shouldn't go
Plumb to Shawnee, to a two-bit rodeo.

The old Ford was a-missin', she jumped and she bucked,
I was fingerin' them coils, a couple was stuck,
She got to hittin' pretty good, after a time
We plowed on through the red clay and slime.

I'd had this old Ford shod up on four new Fisks,
Them thirty by threes about the size of your wrists,
Them new tires wasn't any worry,
They was hunting the highway so we could hurry.

We rolled into Shawnee, it was just gettin' light,
This tribe of Okies was one hell of a sight.
This big fat drunk squaw, and all the sick kids,
And me so damn nervous, about to blow my lid.

I met Homer Todd, he loaned me a five.
Fed all the kids, was lucky to be alive.
I had to give the squaw a slap in the face
'Cause a drunk Indian squaw is a plumb disgrace.

The kids drank a pop, the squaw got a quart,
Threw back her head, and took a big snort.
I won twelve bucks, still don't know where it went,
When we got back home, I didn't have a cent.

Wallace McRae, a rancher from Forsyth, Montana, is known throughout the West as an activist for agricultural concerns. Though just written in 1980, this poem is already considered to be a classic.

REINCARNATION

WALLACE McRAE

What does reincarnation mean?"
A cowpoke ast his friend.
His pal replied, "It happens when
Yer life has reached its end.
They comb yer hair, and warsh yer neck,
And clean yer fingernails,
And lay you in a padded box
Away from life's travails.

"The box and you goes in a hole,
That's been dug into the ground.
Reincarnation starts in when
Yore planted 'neath a mound.
Them clods melt down, just like yer box,
And you who is inside.
And then yore just beginnin' on
Yer transformation ride.

"In a while the grass'll grow
Upon yer rendered mound.
Till some day on yer moldered grave
A lonely flower is found.
And say a hoss should wander by
And graze upon this flower
That once wuz you, but now's become
Yer vegetative bower.

"The posey that the hoss done ate
Up, with his other feed,
Makes bone, and fat, and muscle
Essential to the steed.
But some is left that he can't use
And so it passes through,
And finally lays upon the ground.
This thing, that once wuz you.

"Then say, by chance, I wanders by
And sees this upon the ground,
And I ponders, and I wonders at,
This object that I found.
I thinks of reincarnation,
Of life, and death, and such,
And come away concludin': Slim,
You ain't changed, all that much."

THE LEASE HOUND

WALLACE McRAE

A sharpie in a leisure suit,
With eyelets in his shoes,
Who faintly smelled of talcum
And a little less of booze,
Drove into my neighbor's yard
And gingerly got out,
A little gimpy from the drive,
The altitude, and gout.

He tried to pet their barking dog
While edging to the door,
But once inside his confidence
Sallied to the fore.
"I've come to lease your land for coal,"
Was how he launched his spiel.
He'd been given "authority"
To grant a "generous" deal.

"The nation needs the coal," he said,
"As I am sure you know.
We need more power every year
To make our nation grow.
It's the patriotic duty
Of each American
To help to get the coal mined,
And expedite our plan.

"Now, you may not like strip mining,
And tearing up the earth,
But it's your duty, isn't it,
To the land that gave you birth?
For too long you've reaped the benefits
From places far away.
Your turn has now come up," he said,
"And now, you folks must pay.

"Your power, and the food you eat,
And the lumber in your house,
And all the luxuries you have,
Caused other folks to grouse.
But now your chance has come, at last,
To set the old debt straight.
Just sign the papers I have here,
And you can compensate."

All the time this lecture droned,
My neighbor masked his face.
How could he tell this pompous fool
Their food came from that place;
The lumber came from yonder
North-slope of the hill;
That "make-do" was their motto;
That need meant need, not frill.

The stranger felt he'd seldom
Better delivered his stroke,
He had but to get a signature
From these poor country folk.
His boss would be ecstatic,
His stock would surely rise.
The rutted road, a rainbow,
Had led him to this prize.

He'd do these folks a favor,
Save them from this place.
Though it was dusk, he still had time,
Tonight, a bar to grace.
"If we could have some light," he said,
"You folks could sign the forms.
I could leave here in an hour,
The forecast spoke of storms."

"We won't keep you," said my neighbor,
"No need to stay an hour.
We'll light a lamp to show you out.
You see . . . we don't have no power."

Vess Quinlan is a rancher from Colorado who sold and moved to Tucson, Arizona, where he has been enrolled in poetry classes at the University of Arizona. He writes in both traditional and free forms.

SPRING

VESS QUINLAN

A gentle agony,
Not really painful;
It does not tear,
But nibbles and complains,
Like a child too tired to eat.

I am not frightened or confused.
I know what it is;
Know I can suppress and survive it.
But I should be impatient,
Pushing winter on its way,
       Wanting the brown earth to crawl out
       And awaken from its white sleep.
       I should be looking for tender
       green grass on south slopes,
Worrying about late storms,
Men, tractors, wind,
Wet calves, scours,
And getting heavy ewes in at dark.

I have no worries,
Only an annoying tension growing
Stronger as spring approaches.
It is nearly planting time,
And I am in the city.

The Cowboy Poetry Library which forms the basis of this bibliography was collected with grant funds from the L. J. and Mary C. Skaggs Foundation and the Nevada Humanities Committee, and is permanently housed at the Fife Folklore Archive, Utah State University.

Allen, Francis. *Lone Star Ballads.* Galveston: author-published, 1978.

Allen, Jules Verne. *Cowboy Lore.* New York: The Naylor Co., 1950.

Ashley, Carlos. *That Spotted Sow and Other Hill Country Ballads.* Austin: The Steck Co., 1949.

Barker, Elliot S. *Wilderness, Faith, Action, Humor and Other Poems.* Santa Fe: author-published, 1982.

Barker, S. Omar. *Buckaroo Ballads.* Santa Fe: Santa Fe, New Mexico Publishing Co., 1928.

_____ *Rawhide Rhymes.* Garden City N.Y.: Doubleday & Co., 1968.

_____ *Songs of the Saddlemen.* Denver: Sage Books (Alan Swallow, Publisher), 1954.

Barton, Owen J. *Saddle Talk.* Rogerson, Idaho: author-published, 1984.

Beggs, Wesley. *Rhymes from the Rangeland.* Denver: The Eastwood-Kirchner Printing Co., 1912.

Berg, William. *Poems of the Trail.* Caldwell, Idaho: Caxton Printers, 1949.

Bickley, J. T. H. *The Ghosts of the Chisos.* San Antonio: The Naylor Co., 1950.

Black, Baxter. *The Cowboy and His Dog or Go, Git in the Pickup!* Denver: Record Stockman Press, 1980.

_____ *On the Edge of Common Sense.* Denver: Coyote Cowboy Co. and Record Stockman Press, 1983.

_____ *A Rider, a Roper and a Heck'uva Windmill Man.* Denver: Coyote Cowboy Co. and Record Stockman Press, 1982.

Brewer, Frank A. and Steiner, Francis Brewer. *Ballads of the Book Cliffs.* Fairview, Oreg.: Eastco Print, 1973.

Brininstool, E. A. *Trail Dust of a Maverick.* Los Angeles: Dodd Mead & Co., 1914.

Brisendine, Everett. *Old Cowboys Never Die.* Chino Valley, Ariz.: author-published, 1984.

_____ *One Man of a Kind.* Chino Valley, Ariz.: author-published, 1980.

Brubacher, E.A. *Songs of the Saddle and Trails into Lonesome Land.* Boise: Bess Foster Smith Publisher, n.d.

Campbell, Austin. *Riding the Dim Trail.* Great Falls, Mont.: author-published, 1981.

Carr, Robert V. *Cowboy Lyrics.* Chicago: W. B. Conkey Company, 1908.

Carson, Bob A. *Poems of American Cowboys and Nature.* N.p.: author-published, 1938.

Casteel, Jo. *Cut from the Same Leather.* Vale, S. Dak.: author-published, 1984.

Chapman, Arthur. *Cactus Center.* Cambridge: Houghton Mifflin Co., 1921.

_____ *Out Where the West Begins.* Cambridge: Houghton Mifflin Co., 1917.

Chisolm, Alexander. *The Old Chisolm Trail.* Salt Lake City: Handkraft Art & Publishing Co., 1964.

Chittenden, William Lawrence. *Ranch Verses.* New York: G. P. Putnam's Sons, 1893.

Clark, Badger. *Grass Grown Trails.* New York: Gorham Press, 1917.

_____ *Sun and Saddle Leather.* Boston: Chapman & Grimes, 1942.

Clark, Kenneth, editor, *Songs of the Ranch and Range.* New York: Paull-Pioneer Music Corp., 1932.

Coburn, Wallace D. *Rhymes from a Roundup Camp.* Great Falls, Mont.: W. T. Ridgley Press, 1899.

Countryman, Mark W. *Echoes of the Old West.* New York: The Poetry Digest, 1950.

Crawford, Captain Jack. *The Poet Scout: Verses and Songs.* San Francisco: author-publisher 1879.

_____ *The Bronco Book.* East Aurora, Texas: The Roycrofters, 1908.

Dale, Edward Everett. *The Prairie Schooner and Other Poems.* Guthrie, Okla.: The Co-Operative Publishing Co., 1929.

Davidson, Levette J. *Poems of the Old West.* Denver: The University of Denver Press, 1951.

Dawson, Chet. *A Cowboy's Forty Years of Gathering.* Truth or Consequences, N. Mex.: The Cruse Publishing Co., 1964.

Dean, Delmar. *Ramblings of an Old Cowboy.* Edited by Denise Wheller. Wyo.: author-publisher, 1971.

Devere, William. *Marshall's New Pianner and Other Western Stories.* New York: M. Whitmark & Sons, 1897.

Doramus, Wm. "Bill". *Our Way of Life.* N.p., n.d.

Edison, Carol. *Cowboy Poetry from Utah: an Anthology.* Salt Lake City: Utah Folklife Center, 1985.

Ellard, Harry. *Ranch Tales of the Rockies.* Canon City, Colo.: author-published, 1899.

Ellis, Martha Downer. *Bell Ranch Glimpses,* Conchas Dam, N. Mex.: Ellis Book Co., 1980.

_____ *Rope and Pan.* Clarendon, Texas: Clarendon Press, 1969.

Fife, Austin & Alta. *Ballads of the Great West.* Palo Alto, Calif.: American West Publishing Co., 1970.

_____ *Cowboy and Western Songs.* New York: Bramball House, 1979.

_____ *Heaven on Horseback.* Logan, Utah: Utah State University Press, 1970.

Finger, Charles J. *Frontier Ballads.* Garden City, N.Y.: Doubleday Page & Co., 1927.

Finley, Jewel. *On Desert Trails.* Phoenix: Four Winds Press, 1983.

Fletcher, Bob. *Corral Dust.* Helena, Mont.: State Publishing Co., 1934.

_____ *"Poet Lariat," Prickly Pear Pomes,* Helena, Mont.: Independent Publishing Co., 1920.

Fletcher, Curley W. *Songs of the Sage.* Los Angeles: Frontier Publishing Co., 1931.

Forsgren, Alfred J. *A Powder River Puncher's Poems.* N.p., n.d.

Gardner, Gail I. *Orejana Bull.* Prescott, Ariz.: Prescott Printing Co., 1980.

Goodwyn, Frank. *Poems about the West.* Washington D.C.: Potomac Corral of the Westerners, 1975.

Gough, L. *Spur Jingles and Saddle Songs.* Amarillo, Tex: Russell Stationery Co., 1935.

Gregg, John J. & Barbara T. *Best Loved Poems of the American West.* Garden City, N.Y.: Doubleday & Co., 1980.

Griggs, Nathan Kirk. *Lyrics of the Lariat.* Chicago: Fleming H. Revell Co., 1893.

Haas, Chuck. *Rhymes o' a Driftin' Cowboy.* Flagstaff, Ariz.: Northland Press, 1969.

Halsell, H. H. *Memories of Old Time Chisholm Trail.* Lubbock, Tex: author-published, n.d.

Hamm, W. Howard. *Trail Dust #1.* N.p.: author-published, 1981.

_____ *Trail Dust #2.* N.p.: author-published, 1981.

Hamner, Laura V. *Prairie Vagabonds.* San Antonio: The Naylor Co., 1955.

Handley, Herbert (Jake). *Old Hands and Old Brands.* Windsor, Colo.: Coren Printing, 1981.

Hanson, Joseph Mills. *Frontier Ballads.* Chicago: A. C. McClurg & Co., 1910.

Harkness, Samuel. *Horse-Thief Gulch.* Kingsport, Tenn.: J. H. Sears & Co., 1928.

Heckle, Texas B. *Rhymes of the Frontier: Volume II.* N.p.: The Arizona Printers, 1929.

Hersey, Harold. *Singing Rawhide.* New York: George H. Doran Co., 1926.

Higgins, Pecos & Evans, Joe. *Pecos' Poems.* El Paso: author-published, 1956.

Hookham, Claude. *Rambling Thoughts in Homespun Verse.* Emigrant, Mont.: author-published, 1960.

Horan, Jack. *Burnt Leather.* Boston: Christopher Publishing, 1937.

Hughes, Joe. *An Old Bitter Rooter's Thoughts in Poetry.* Hamilton, Mont.: Bitter Root Valley Historical Society, 1981.

Hurd, Harry Elmore. *West of Eden.* Boston: author-published, 1934.

Jameson, Laurance Lincoln. *Cow Country Ballads.* Casper, Wyo.: Prairie Publishing Co., 1941.

Jennings, Jim. *Tumble Weed.* Helena, Mont.: State Publishing Co., 1956.

Johnson, Nick. *Wind River Poems.* Pabsco-Globe, Ariz.: Anne Johnson Deal, Publisher, 1957.

Johnston, Bob. *Stories and Poems.* Scottsbluff, Neb.: M. W. Nichols & Assoc., 1984.

King, Olephia ("Leafy"). *Western Poems.* Fallon, Nev.: Fallon Publishing Co., 1966.

_____ *Western Poems No. 2.* Fallon, Nev.: Fallon Publishing Co., 1967.

Kiskaddon, Bruce. *Rhymes of the Ranges.* Hollywood: Earl Hayes, 1924.

_____ *Rhymes of the Ranges and Other Poems.* Los Angeles: Heitman Printing Co., 1947.

_____ *Western Poems.* Los Angeles: Western Livestock Journal, 1935.

Knibbs, Henry Herbert. *Riders of the Stars.* Cambridge: Houghton Mifflin Co., 1916.

_____ *Songs of the Lost Frontier.* Cambrige: Houghton Mifflin Co., 1930.

_____ *Songs of the Outland.* Cambridge: Houghton Mifflin Co., 1914.

_____ *Songs of the Trail.* Cambridge: Houghton Mifflin Co., 1920.

Lambert, Fred. *Bygone Days of the Old West.* N.p.: Burton Publishing Co., 1948.

Lane, Wade. *Cowboy Meditations.* N.p.: Suttonhouse Ltd., 1936.

Larkin, Margaret. *Singing Cowboy.* New York: Alfred A. Knopf, 1931.

Lee, "Powder River" Jack H. and Kitty. *Cowboy Wails and Cattle Trails.* Butte, Mont.: The McKee Printing Co., 1936.

_____ *The Stampede.* Greensburg, Penn.: Standardized Press, before 1941.

Lee, Katie. *Ten Thousand Goddam Cattle.* Flagstaff, Ariz.: Northland Press, 1976.

Lemon, Frank D. *More Rhymes of a Ranch Hand.* Moab, Utah: Times-Independent Printing, 1975.

Lewis, Rosell. *Memories of the XIT.* San Antonio: The Naylor Co., 1960.

Lincoln, Elliot C. *The Ranch.* Cambridge: Houghton Mifflin Co., 1924.

_____ *Rhymes of a Homesteader.* Cambridge: Houghton Mifflin Co., 1920.

Lingenfelter, Richard E. and Dwyer, Richard A. *Songs of the American West.* Los Angeles: University of California Press, 1968.

Lively, W. Irven. *Ananias of Arizona.* Phoenix: author-published, 1953.

_____ *Camp and Trail,* N.p., n.d.

Lomax, John A. *Cowboy Songs.* New York: The Macmillan Co., 1910.

_____ *Songs of the Cattle Trail and Cow Camp.* New York: The Macmillan Co., 1919.

Lummis, Charles F. *A Bronco Pegasus.* Cambridge: Houghton Mifflin Co., 1928.

McArthur, J'Wayne and McKendrick, Scott. *The Cowboy.* Logan, Utah: author-published, 1978.

McCoy, T. J. (Tim). *Day Dreams of a Nighthawk.* Wyo.: N.p., c. 1921.

McGrady, Don. *Firewater and Gas.* Chicago: Adams Press, 1972.

McRae, Wallace. *It's Just Grass and Water.* Spokane, Wash.: Shawn Higgins, Publisher, 1979.

_____ *Up North is Down the Creek.* Helena, Mont.: Museum of the Rockies, 1985.

Mahoney, Timothy. *Wyoming's Rancher Poet.* Compiled by Tom Nicholas. Casper, Wyo.: Central Rocky Mountain Co., 1983.

Major, Mabel and Pearce, T. M. *Signature of the Sun.* Albuquerque: The University of New Mexico Press, 1950.

Markley, John R. *Too Thick to Drink . . . Too Thin to Plow: Poems of the Cow Country.* N.p.: author-published, 1984.

Martin, Gage. *Corral Dust.* N.p.: author-publisher, 1947.

Miller, E. W. "Roy". *Thoughts in Rhyme.* Freeman, S. Dak.: Pine Hill Press, 1980.

_____ *Thoughts in Rhyme Volume II.* Freeman, S. Dak.: Pine Hill Press, n.d.

Montana Folklife Project. *When the Work's All Done This Fall: Songs, Stories, and Poems from Montana Cattle Camps and Cow Trails.* (L.P. and notes) Helena, Mont.: Montana Arts Council, 1982.

Munson, Marjorie Sawyer. *Muleshoe Ballads of Oklahoma Bob.* Alva, Okla.: Maxwell Printing Co., 1944.

Norskog, Howard L. *Passing Through.* Powell, Wyo.: author-published, 1982.

Ohrlin, Glenn. *The Hell-Bound Train, A Cowboy Songbook.* Urbana, Ill.: University of Illinois Press, 1973.

O'Malley, D. J. *D. J. O'Malley, Cowboy Poet.* Ean Claire, Wis.: author-published, 1934.

Pecoraro, Irene and Whitehead, Blondell. *Partners in Poetry.* Lander, Wyo.: author-published, 1979.

Piper, Edwin Ford. *Barbed Wire and Other Poems.* Iowa City, Iowa: The Midland Press, 1919.

Potter, Edgar R. *Whoa . . . Ya Sonsabitches.* Havre, Mont.: Griggs Publishing Co., 1977.

Raley, Tom. *Rodeo Fever.* Phoenix: Latigo Press, 1979.

Ralston, James Kenneth. *Rhymes of a Cowboy.* Billings, Mont.: Blueprint & Letter Co., 1972.

Randolph, Col. Charles D. *Western Poems.* N.p.: author-published, 1925.

Ritch, Johnny. *Horsefeathers.* Helena, Mont.: author-published, 1941.

Robertson, Clyde. *Pony Nelson and Other Western Ballads.* New York: Exposition Press, 1954.

Ross, Bob. *Muddled Meanderings in an Outhouse.* N.p.: author-published, 1970.

Ross, "Country Don". *Roads I've Traveled.* N.p.: Pal Industries, 1983.

Russell, Charles M. *Good Medicine.* New York: Doubleday & Co., 1966.

Ryan, Phillip. *Now and Then.* Houston: Kel-Tec, Inc., 1981.

Sarrett, Lew. *Slow Smoke.* New York: Henry Holt & Co., 1925.

Shipp, E. Richard. *Intermountain Folk: Songs of Their Days and Ways.* Casper, Wyo.: Casper Stationery Co., 1922.

_____ *Rangeland Melodies.* Casper, Wyo.: Casper Stationery Co., 1923.

Sicking, Georgie Connell. *Just Thinkin.* Fallon, Nev.: author-published, n.d.

Simpson, William Haskell. *Along Old Trails.* Cambridge: Houghton Mifflin Co., 1929.

Sloan, H. D. *Rancher's Writings.* N.p., n.d.

Smith, Don Ian. *Ranchland Poems.* Boise, Idaho: Larson Printing, 1980.

Smith, Lawrence B. (Lon). *The Sunlight Kid and Other Western Verses.* New York: E. P. Dutton & Co., 1935.

Smith, Shep. *Sawdust & Shavings.* N.p., n.d.

Stevenson, James H. *Songs & Poems of the Old West by an Old Cowboy.* N.p.: 1937.

Targ, William. *The American West.* Cleveland: The World Publishing Co., 1946.

Taylor, Gene. *Chips of Thought.* Farmington, N. Mex.: The Print Shop, 1982.

Thorp, N. Howard (Jack). *Pardner of the Wind.* Lincoln: University of Nebraska Press, 1977.

_____ *Songs of the Cowboy.* Estancia, N. Mex.: News Print Shop, 1908.

Tinsley, Jim Bob. *He Was Singin' This Song.* Orlando: University of Central Florida, 1981.

Underwood, John Curtis. *Trails End.* Santa Fe: New Mexican Publishing Corp., 1921.

Warner, Charles. *Old Coins of the Sweet Grass Hills.* Kalispell, Mont.: Thomas Printing Co., 1965.

Westermeier, Clifford P. *Trailing the Cowboy.* Caldwell, Idaho: The Caxton Printers, 1955.

Whilt, Jim. *Mountain Echoes.* Kalispell, Mont.: The O'Neil Printers, 1951.

White, John I. *Git Along Little Doagies.* Urbana: University of Illinois Press, 1975.

Whitehead, Blondell. *Blondell's Ballads and Folklore.* Lander, Wyo.: author-published, 1978.

Wild, Everett. *The Western Poems of Everett Wild.* Phoenix: author-published, N.d.

Wilhelm, Stephen R. *Cowboy Poet.* N.p.: author-published, 1949.

Wilkerson, Buck. *Day Dreams and Memories of the Old West.* N.p.: author-published, 1971.

Wilson, Joe "Blackie". *Bell Bottoms to Boots.* Freer, Texas: The Freer Enterprise, 1938.

Wiltbank, Milo. *Whiff of the West.* San Antonio: The Naylor Co., 1973.

Wirries, Mary Mabel. *Roped and Tied.* Phoenix: Goldenetz Bros. Printing Co., 1945.

"'Bueno, Which in Spanish Means Good" © 1985 by Nyle A. Henderson

"How Many Cows?" © 1985 by Nyle A. Henderson

"Ol' Edgar Martin" © 1985 by Carlos Ashley

"To Be a Top Hand" © 1985 by Georgie Sicking

"Old Tuff" © 1985 by Georgie Sicking

"For Jeff" © 1985 by Jon Bowerman

"Tribute to Freckles and Tornado" © 1985 by Jon Bowerman

"Grey's River Roundup" © 1985 by Howard Norskog

"The Book" © 1985 by Waddie Mitchell

"The Throw-back" © 1985 by Waddie Mitchell

"One Red Rose" © 1985 by Ernie Fanning

"The Vanishing Valley" © 1985 by Ernie Fanning

"Saturday Night in Woody" © 1985 by Jesse Smith

"Saddle Tramp" © 1985 by Buck Wilkerson

"The Kid Solos" © 1985 by Bob Schild

"Two of a Kind" © 1985 by Bob Schild

"Matching Green Ribbon" © 1985 by Jim Hofer

"A Time to Stay, a Time to Go" © 1985 by Baxter Black

"The Big High and Lonesome" © 1985 by Baxter Black

"Poets Gathering, 1985" © 1985 by Charles Kortes

"Greasin' the Miles" © 1985 by Nick Johnson

"Dudes" © 1985 by Nick Johnson

"Bellerin' and Bawlin'" © 1985 by Linda Ash

"The Great Wanagan Creek Flood" © 1985 by Bill Lowman

"So Long" © 1985 by Ross Knox

"Easy Chairs and Saddle Sores" © 1985 by Ross Knox

"The Dying Times" © 1985 by Ross Knox

"Open Range" © 1985 by Melvin L. Whipple

"Old Horse" © 1985 by Don Ian Smith